21°48' ~ 22°27'N　113°03' ~ 114°19'E

珠　海
MULTIFACETED
ZHUHAI
CHINA

五洲传播出版社
China Intercontinental Press

Zhū

珠海

hăi
ON THE WORLD STAGE

To anyone who has fal

Presented by
珠 海 市 人 民 政 府 新 闻 办 公 室
Information Office of Zhuhai Municipal People's Government

n in love with a city

Produced by
五洲传播出版社 《城市漫步》 全国英文刊
China Intercontinental Press / that's China (magazine)

zhuhai 珠海杂志社有限公司
Zhuhai Magazine Co., Ltd.

Zhuhai Impressions
A Humanist Perspective

by Leo Ou-fan LEE 李歐梵 (Hong Kong)

Zhuhai—literally "a sea of pearls" in Chinese—is a city situated at the southern tip of China across a narrow river from neighboring Macao. Transformed by designation as a Special Economic Zone in 1980, this growing, modern city is well-known for recently established universities, golf resorts, terrific infrastructure, theme parks, and islands off the Pearl River Delta. But this description does little to portray the real charm and true nature of the area. Recently, a friend shared this much more human description:

Zhuhai is like a quiet friend who is not pretentious and does not have a self-inflating ego. Zhuhai loves books and knows how to live and is certainly not the kind of aggressive moneymaker you meet in many other cities. Residents of this city seem to have a different temperament. After deciding to settle down and make Zhuhai their home, they blatantly pursue a peaceful and comfortable lifestyle, rather than simply a hefty bank account.

It is an open secret that more and more people—and not merely retirees—have been attracted by the city's high quality of life. The current population has gone beyond 1.89 million, which makes Zhuhai no longer a small-sized border town but a developing, modern city. In a way, Zhuhai and Macao can well be seen as twin cities parallel to Shenzhen and Hong Kong. But here the uniqueness of Zhuhai shines through in the way that it provides a leisurely pace and a general sense of wellbeing. Zhuhai is a port city with unrivalled oceanic scenery where the Pearl River flows into the sea. One of the city's major scenic attractions is a north-south shoreline highway lined with palm, banyan and other tropical trees. Appropriately called "Love Promenade", it seems earmarked for leisurely strolling. One can hear the sound of waves beating on the beaches. The quiet romantic atmosphere makes a sharp contrast to the hustle and bustle of other port cities nearby.

Zhuhai, the modern and burgeoning city, has yet to define its identity. Will it become another trade center for loading and unloading goods, or a vacation resort with its golf courses and theme parks, or something else? Though a small township in old times, Zhuhai was one of the earliest ports to be exposed to Western influence. The greater Zhuhai area can claim both Sun Yat-sen, the leader of the Republican Revolution (who was born in a village nearby) and Yung Wing, the first Chinese to graduate from an American university, as its native sons. History has also left its dark traces. During the Opium Wars in the mid-19th century, the nearby sea passages were the sites of opium trade and some fierce skirmishes between China and Great Britain.

At the present moment, however, Zhuhai is poised for a grand plan: the development of the Greater Bay Area. It is one of the nine cities in the Chinese mainland that form the central nexus to be linked by super highways and the recently opened Hong Kong-Zhuhai-Macao Bridge, which will inevitably speed up the city's economic development.

For a city that prides itself on its scenic beauty and the quality of life, its future development offers both an opportunity and a challenge. Let's hope that this "pearl in the sea" will continue to be blessed by its good location, good people, and good values.

TOP PICKS

- **THE BLUEPRINT** (p033)　It was the first time PMO named an asteroid after a Chinese city. In a similar manner as this astronomical object orbiting the Sun, its namesake—Zhuhai—is like a new star in the universe that was rediscovered in 1979.
- **DRAGON ON THE SEA** (p040)　Judging by the bridge's sheer size and architectural scope, Zhuhai is surely a city on the move; ambitious, forward thinking, and not afraid to make a statement.
- **A CITY ON WINGS** (p055)　Designed by Liu Thai Ker, the master planner of Singapore, Jinwan is designed for the future in the true sense of the word.
- **AN ODE TO THE RIGHTEOUS AND THE HEROIC** (p089)　Tong Shao-yi's real-life romance, adventure and indefinably charming charisma seems to out-distance any posthumous attempt at evaluation or praise.
- **THE GAP ROCK LIGHTHOUSE** (p108)　The history of this rare piece of "built heritage" embodies the collaboration between different, often fiercely competing entities at a level that was precedent-setting.
- **THE LOVE PROMENADE** (p117)　No one visiting Zhuhai should leave the city without checking out the Love Promenade, created with (and married to) the city's golden coastline.
- **DECIDEDLY SPORTY** (p131)　The city is decidedly sporty, drawing Stefanie Graf for its openness and growing power embodied in the WTA Elite Trophy and harnessing the glare of the world's media.
- **IT HAS TO BE...THE ISLANDS** (p160)　This city's uniquely rich, island resources and coastline of nearly 700 kilometers extend far beyond what one solitary trip can offer if one truly wants to savor the region's unrivalled coastal beauty.
- **ZHUHAI'S EVER-EXPANDING PARKLAND GRID** (p214)　Zhuhai's "greensward plan" has virtually turned the whole city into an extended, inter-connected parkland.
- **A PARADISE FOR ALL** (p246)　This elaborately built garden is an architectural treasure that reflects both Tong Shao-yi's highly developed aesthetics fostered by the man's Chinese roots and the western part of his soul.
- **QIXIA XIANGUAN** (p260)　The most eloquent and touching expression of Huitong Village's mystique is the "Wuthering Heights of Zhuhai", haunting, romantic and brooding.
- **DOUMEN OLD STREET** (p267)　Walking under the colorful, exotic window lattices now feels pleasantly anachronistic.
- **CREATIVE BEISHAN** (p321)　Here, tradition is not ossified, but feted along with innovation and joie de vivre.

GEM OF A CITY

086

267

275

260-261

165

HISTORIC

088

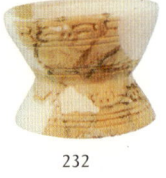
363

291

066

083

232

248

237

040-041

170

089

300

293

194

CULTURE

284-285

105

268-269

192

091

250

177

ISLAND

109

188-189

199

182

356-357

354-355

126

JOIE DE VIVRE

DELICIOUS

257

322

308

374

391

337

326

338-339

382

MODERN

384

399

353

372

392-393

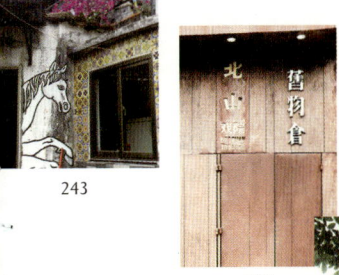

306-307

132

130

243

332

SPORTY

150-151

120

146-147

341

135

ZHUHAI THROUG

People from far and wide who have traveled to Zhuhai tell how they fell in love with this inimitable city.

THROUGH FOREIGN EYES

Roser Cervera

LOVE AT FIRST SIGHT

ZHUHAI THROUGH FOREIGN EYES

NATIONALITY: Spanish

11 years in Zhuhai (2007-2018), Senior Lecturer and Spanish Subjects Convenor,

United International College

As I am sitting at the Nanhai Oil (Zhuhai) Hotel looking at my son playing tennis under a beautiful blue sky with white clouds, I think of how much he has grown this past year and how different is his childhood compared to mine. He is eight years old, speaks four languages and has a great multicultural environment to learn from.

I was born in one of the musical centers of Catalonia, Igualada, a northeastern city of Spain near Barcelona where Catalan and Spanish cultures intersect. I entered school at the age of two where I developed a caring nature, and my passion for teaching, languages, different cultures and music. Fresh in my memory, I still have vivid images of a little version of me helping my "slower learning" classmates to finish their tasks and defending those who were bullied. I went a few times to the Headmaster's office because of that, and enjoyed the songs we learned at school from around the world in different languages.

As a classically trained musician, I have also enjoyed exposure to the diverse musical heritage of Europe, Asia and the New World both as a soloist and in different music ensembles thanks to my voice and my violin. Music made me travel, travel made me learn foreign languages, and learning foreign languages made me understand different cultures. As Nelson Mandela said: "If you talk to a man in a language he understands, that goes to his head. If you talk to him in his language, that goes to his heart". That has been part of my philosophy of life and something that I try to instill in all my students. Sometimes I fail.

I still remember when I first came to Zhuhai for a job interview in 2007. I arrived at the University Campus Area where Beijing Institute of Technology, Zhuhai, and Beijing Normal University, Zhuhai are located, under a blue sky like today's. Same sky, same time of the year. Suddenly, it was like someone had opened a "tap" in the sky and all the water was giving life to the palette of color that I was admiring from the bus window: the trees, the plants, the flowers... Then, the door opened and I felt in my body the weight of humidity and the scent of the soil after the rain. What a beautiful welcome. Zhuhai had something special.

I walked along Jinfeng Road under centuries-old, majestic trees which were decapitated by the typhoon last summer. Then, at the top of that small road, there was a beautiful building, United International College (UIC), an English Medium Liberal Arts College that had just opened. For the first time in China, I did not feel illiterate, I could understand what was written because it was in English. After meeting many interesting professors from all over the globe, enjoying their fantastic stories, and speaking in some of the languages that I have mastered, I knew I wanted to become one of the characters

Then, I met Zhuhai, and as what happens when you fall in love with someone, Zhuhai became a part of me.

of that book.

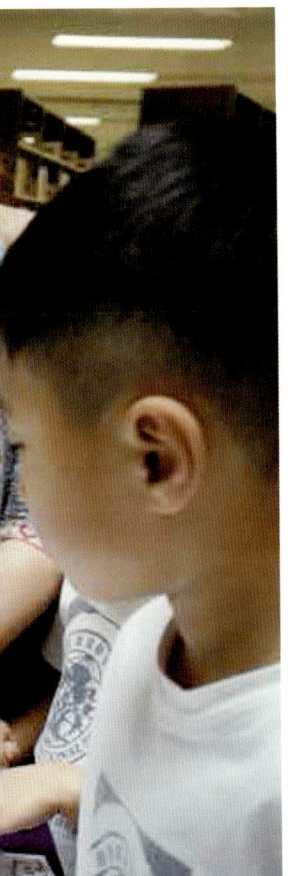

Prior to Zhuhai, I was the Academic Director of the French Program at South China Normal University until I discovered, by serendipity, UIC. Most of my colleagues and friends did not understand why I left that position to become a "simple" lecturer and start a new language section. True educators do not need diplomas, positions or titles to excel in what they do. It is funny how, often times, we adults tend to pay so much attention to titles, positions, numbers, and appearance, rather than concentrate on the simplest things that life offers us. Antoine de Saint-Exupery teaches us in *The Little Prince*: "What is important is invisible to the eyes." Thanks to that decision, my life has been fulfilled with multicultural friends and colleagues, concerts and musicians, and great opportunities to excel and share my knowledge. But it has also given me the chance to explore parts of the city like the Putuo Temple, and more recently, Huitong Village where our new campus is located. These are two very special spots where you will grasp some of the special feeling which I have towards this city.

When I close my eyes, I can see as if in slow motion, all the transformations that have occurred over the past decade. This city has evolved at an incredible speed to accommodate the addition of more cars, more people, more buildings, which include the astonishing engineering masterpiece of the Hong Kong-Zhuhai-Macao Bridge, the Zhuhai Hengqin International Tennis Centre where the WTA tournament is held every year, and the Zhuhai Opera House standing on Yeli Island as the newest landmark for a city that is thirsty for cultural events. Zhuhai is continuously creating more spaces to develop the growing demand for culture, sports and education. I do hope that we can still preserve the environment and its green spaces during this process. I came to China to learn about its ancient culture and Chinese language but, above all, I came to contribute to developing foreign languages, culture and music education. Then, I met Zhuhai, and as what happens when you fall in love with someone, Zhuhai became a part of me. I hope I am making a positive, long-lasting contribution to education in the place that has become a home away from home.

Andrew VanderMeulen

ADVENTURES AND HAPPINESS

ZHUHAI THROUGH FOREIGN EYES

NATIONALITY: Canadian
1 year (2017-2018),
Principal of ZIS (Zhuhai International School)

Seeing Zhuhai through the eyes of others refreshes your perspective and experience of the city. How quickly we grow accustomed to, and take for granted, the welcoming climate, the spacious boulevards, and the hospitable welcome of the still nascent city that is rapidly defining itself and rising to its place in the Pearl River Delta. Thankfully it only takes a tour with guests to remember one's own first fond and hopeful impressions of this place.

This month marks the first anniversary of my family's first arrival to Zhuhai. After four years of life in Shanghai, the opportunity to relocate to Zhuhai International School as Head of School presented itself. We knew we were leaving behind one of the world's great metropolises, but from our first glimpse of Zhuhai as we followed the coastal highway we had no doubts that this place had adventures and happiness in store for us.

As is true in any career, in education it is far too easy to become so immersed in work that one's sense of time and place fades to the background. Dutifully, when guests arrive, my parents in fact, the obligation as host and guide takes over, forcing eyes and mind open to the sights and sounds of the city once again. Our first destination was Qi'ao Island on the north end of the city. They wanted to see the school campus, and as we drove onto the island the sounds of the birdlife and the wind in the trees welcomed us in a way I had too easily grown accustomed to hearing. The beachside restaurants proved irresistible, wafting their seafood barbeque temptations through our open windows, mixing deliciously with the sea breeze. Still today, I am thankful to having experienced the commute to school through fresh eyes. I can now draw on the memories of my parents' exclamations at the island's beauty and their impressions of the 360-degree view of downtown Zhuhai, Hong Kong, Macao, and Shenzhen from the rooftop of our school.

Our main goal for the rest of our tour of Zhuhai was to see as much as possible on foot or by bicycle. Tangjia Town proved to be a perfect destination to absorb the life of Zhuhai. Wandering through the old village along Shanfang Road we enjoyed the blend of new and ancient. Making our way to the old wet market, the bustle of the afternoon shopping kept us entertained as we joined the flow of preparations for the evening. Our tour of the city continued with a serene day at Putuo Temple in Xiangzhou District, and the architecture, colours, and sounds of the active temple far exceeded our expectations. We felt privileged to witness and share in the living and breathing of a culture far removed from a traditional Canadian upbringing.

A less welcome guest arrived at Zhuhai's shores in August, 2017 as Typhoon Hato stretched itself over the city. The response of volunteerism that met the damage and destruction of the storm revealed the character of the city residents. Teams of neighbours rallied together

to pick up what debris they could, sharing work gloves as readily as their recounts of the wind and driving rain. This community response, motivated to restore the beauty of their landscape and neighbourhood, peeled away the notion of being an expat in a foreign country and revealed a shared sense of pride in and care for the place we call home. In a way, Zhuhai was given a choice with the storm: either to relent or to show resolve and commitment to the vision for the city. The volunteers and the response teams gave the answer plainly—Zhuhai would persist in spirit and in structure.

I feel fortunate to spend the school days in an international setting with over twenty nationalities on campus each day. Living and teaching abroad for nearly fifteen years, my notion of community has come to encompass the diversity that is the mosaic of an international school. And when such a community is surrounded by a lively, caring, and proud city, then I can't help myself but to be full of hope and a sense of belonging.

From our first glimpse of Zhuhai as we followed the coastal highway we had no doubts that this place had adventures and happiness in store for us.

Frank Bodenhage

LIFE AND WORK IN ZHUHAI

NATIONALITY: German

12 years in Zhuhai (2006-2018), former Director of MTU Maintenance Zhuhai

Today I'm sitting in my office, enjoying the rest time during lunch and between two meetings in a busy schedule. It is 2018 now and after a long period of sunny and hot days, rain came back as a typhoon is approaching Guangdong province.

Soon I'll be leaving the city, back to my home country thousands of miles away, together with my loving wife and our two kids. Time to pack and prepare, but also to look back.

Switching back to 2006, the year I arrived in Zhuhai, is not easy. The pace of life and change has been very quick, filled with lots of changes, developments, experiences and many more aspects—so the memory gets more distant. Life and work here was pretty different then.

Zhuhai by then was already a quite big city, but in Chinese measures it still was countryside. Hardly any people spoke English and I also yet had to start learning Chinese. Our company had already operated for several years, but staff and business were still quite limited. There weren't many cars on the streets and the areas like Huafa Century City were empty. On the way out to (GDFTZ) Hengqin, there were hardly any buildings after leaving Wanzai, and when going to Hengqin Island it was to enjoy the oysters from one of the barbecue stalls along the road to the small village.

I liked it.

Soon I met my girlfriend and later wife and we grew a family, with our two kids born here. My center of life moved to Zhuhai and till today I'm very happy every day. I was lucky enough that my employer agreed to extend my contract several times, so 2 years became 4, then 6, then 8, 10 and ultimately 12 years.

As our family grew, so did and does Zhuhai. Over these years that I've been here, it must have at least doubled in size and population. And there is no end in sight. There are new museums, conference centers, cultural centers, companies and residential buildings—finished and under construction. At the same time, the infrastructure is continuously upgraded, whilst in many areas it can still not keep pace with the ever increasing number of cars.

The whole development of Hengqin New Area is massively impressive as it was a quite remote place before. Now it's already transformed and keeps transforming.

The biggest of it all, however, might be the Hong Kong-Zhuhai-Macao Bridge. The longest of its kind in the world, it joins Zhuhai with the cosmopolitan world of Hong Kong and beyond. Depending on how easy and conveniently the bridge can finally be used, that for sure will have a big impact on Zhuhai. Previously at the "end" of the Pearl River Delta towards its less economically developed west, it suddenly gets directly integrated into it.

That—combined with the aim to develop the Guangdong-Hong Kong-Macao Greater Bay Area—will drive the next decades of development for Zhuhai and the region.

Besides all these positive aspects it also brings disadvantages, challenges and burden. High attention has to be paid to protect Zhuhai's image as a place to do good business, but also relax. Development will hopefully not destroy and cover all the green areas and wild land around Zhuhai and it can grow within it.

I'll be leaving Zhuhai at the end of this month and am already looking forward to visiting again soon. I hope I will have the chance to see Zhuhai growing bigger and more beautiful. I'm thankful for the experience gained here and will with my family always carry that in our memories.

A CITY OF LEARNING

Victor J. Rodriguez

NATIONALITY: American

Associate Professor of History at Sino-U.S. College (SUC, BITZH) in Zhuhai.

"You won't be challenged," one friend advised me when I shared with him that I would travel to China to teach. It was the summer of 2010 and, even at that time, there seemed to still be among some scholar friends a distorted view that most Asian nations were a good place to witness history—"the rise of China"— or grow spiritually, but not to grow intellectually, and reflected the old "Orientalist" bias. But my instincts told me otherwise—as well as my training as a historian—and that summer I accepted an offer to teach at UIC (United International College), a new institution of higher learning that had been founded recently in the southern city of Zhuhai. I had just graduated with a doctoral degree in History from UCLA and, after two years of teaching in Virginia and Oregon in the United States, I yearned for something different. In fact, I yearned specifically for the kind of challenge that this new university promised: a new style of education—activity-based, socially-engaged, and intellectually challenging—to complement the new trends in China.

I arrived in Zhuhai and quickly learned how the city was positioning itself as a city of learning. UIC stood out as one of several institutions providing an international setting for their students. In particular, it stood out as a champion of creativity in learning and thought. As a faculty member, I was happy to join in promoting new methods of learning that would challenge the student's traditional penchant for sheer memorization of material and encourage the new goal for students: to become practical citizens of the world, continuously moving the nation forward. On the one hand, it was true: I did encounter students who could memorize entire passages from textbooks and reproduce them as answers to my questions. However, I also observed that, on the other hand, the reason for this over-reliance on memorization was that the highly creative faculties of students, so evident in daily life, were not sufficiently reinforced in school. This was complicated by a great fear of being wrong; being wrong meant getting a low grade, which could mean disaster for their future academic careers. So, an important task for me, with the support of my university and the forward movement of modern Chinese culture, was to encourage risking failure; to imagine school not just as a competitive cauldron but also as an adventurous place where failure led to learning, not punishment. We needed to connect the faculties so natural to the students in other aspects of their lives to these new, university-level, learning methods.

I was surprised to discover that, in order to build this bridge, as a faculty I had to do the same, but in reverse: connect my learning to their lives. And thus began a wonderful process of mutual understanding and sharing, which was facilitated by another discovery: the strong bond that students make with their mentors in China. In meeting families, traveling to hometowns, and sharing meals, this deepening of appreciation continued and will now last a lifetime for all of us. This educational process defined my first relationship with Zhuhai, the city where I work and live. During my first years, my teaching duties consumed most of my time and I came to understand Zhuhai purely in terms of learning. Zhuhai's fame as a green city with clean air and a concern for a healthy environment served as a perfect scenario, though. In fact, learning and environmentalism were two intertwined aspects of one urban reality: a city that encouraged exploration, valued knowledge and rewarded innovation. Subsequently, this dimension of the city served as a bridge for me to explore the multiple localities that were gathered to create Zhuhai as a city. Along with my students and colleagues, we came to know what were, at least for me, urban worlds that predated Zhuhai's modern incarnations and which were being transformed vertiginously. This engendered a second relationship with Zhuhai—with its many local cultural expressions—and prefigures for me a second project, perhaps one more challenging than the first: to learn its local histories. As a work-in-progress, it is oftentimes limited by the difficulties of learning Cantonese. I still live in a translated world, mostly in an English-speaking world, but one enhanced by my progress in Mandarin Chinese.

Do I regret coming to Zhuhai? Absolutely not. My stay here—now 6 years—has been productive. I have formed relationships that will last a lifetime. I feel I have been part of the city's history, even if just a tiny part. Do I miss home? Oftentimes. I especially miss the theater, not just big-budget productions, but the popular theater, the college theater, the theater that springs forth from the people. I wish we could have more of that in Zhuhai. But given that Zhuhai's great asset is its people—especially the extraordinary variety of people from all parts of China that live here, I expect extraordinary changes to happen as a result. It feels great to be part of this story of learning and growing.

Andrew Webb-Mitchell

MY MUSICAL LIFE IN ZHUHAI

ZHUHAI THROUGH FOREIGN EYES

NATIONALITY: British

Composer, Music Director, British Schools Foundation Choral Programme

MY MUSICAL LIFE IN ZHUHAI

The elegant outline of Zhuhai Opera House's two shell-shaped structures dominates the coastal skyline and has started to symbolise the city, perhaps indicating something of its cultural ambitions. In this context, it is easy to understand why a British arts organisation might choose Zhuhai to launch a choral programme. Zhuhai's relatively small size in comparison with the neighbouring cities of Shenzhen and Guangzhou, its close proximity to Macao and Hong Kong, its clean environment, excellent transport links and most of all its well-educated and affluent population all serve to make it an attractive proposition. In addition, Zhuhai's cultural life, still in early stages of development, coupled with an excellent infrastructure for the arts, leads to the inevitable conclusion that it has great potential for providers of high level arts education.

In September 2018, Zhuhai Classical Children's Choir began a three-year tenure as Choir-in-Residence at Zhuhai Opera House. Such residences are extremely rare in China and this one came as the result of an invitation from Poly Education who is launching an education centre within the opera house with the aim of becoming a hub for arts and culture in the region.

Zhuhai Classical Children's Choir's association with Zhuhai Opera House dates back to the opera house's inaugural concerts in December 2016, when the choir performed works by Tchaikovsky and Borodin with the Russian National Orchestra conducted by Shostakovich's erstwhile friend, Thomas Sanderling. As of September 2018, the choir is now able to enjoy the rich cultural environment of the opera house on a weekly basis for rehearsals and regularly performs there.

I founded the choir in May 2013 as founding ensemble of the British Schools Foundation Choral Programme, and since then we have endeavoured to build a reputation for performing challenging classical repertoire at prestigious venues. Since making its professional debut in December 2015, singing Johann Strauss's *Tritch-Tratch Polka* at the Changsha Concert Hall with Zubin Mehta and the Israel Philharmonic Orchestra, the choir has performed regularly throughout China. A few days following their debut, the choir performed with Sinfonietta Cracovia in Zhongshan Culture and Art Centre. In November 2017, the choir performed *Byrd Mass in Three Parts* at the Central Conservatory of

Music in Beijing as part of the International Chamber Music Festival. The concert was subsequently broadcast on China Central Television (CCTV).

In March 2017, the choir provided the challenging off-stage chorus for a performance of Holst Planets Suite with Guiyang Symphony Orchestra conducted by Rico Sacanni. The choir then returned to Guiyang the following June to perform Puccini's *Madama Butterfly* with renowned Chinese opera stars, Li Xiuying and Liang Ning. Zhuhai Classical Children's Choir made their first overseas appearance in October 2016, singing for HRH Princess Anne at the British School of Kuala Lumpur. Performances of such challenging works are testimony, if any were needed, to the astonishing aptitude, stamina and ambition of Chinese children and an indication of their willingness to embrace and master music from other cultures.

The British Schools Foundation is a UK-registered, non-profit organisation and a leading international school group. Having founded 10 schools in eight countries across three continents, including the British Schools of Beijing, Guangzhou and Nanjing, the British Schools Foundation launched the choral programme with the aim of promoting the benefits of British education and culture within the broader Chinese community. The choral programme provides conservatory-standard musical training in the English choral tradition to children aged between 8 and 18. Choristers rehearse secular and sacred choral works in a variety of original languages, including English, Latin, Italian and German. There is a great emphasis on high standards of discipline and independent study, with high expectations for attendance and punctuality. The choristers wear a formal uniform and stand throughout each two-hour rehearsal. Rehearsals take place in smaller-scale classes based on ability, with each class named after a British composer of choral music; Byrd, Purcell, Parry, Elgar and Britten. Each chorister is expected to practice individually and they are assessed on performances of their vocal part, recorded at home and then submitted to the choral centre. Only choristers with a high assessment grade are eligible to participate in concerts. This somewhat rigid and highly structured approach ensures that every chorister on stage has mastered the music and can face the public with great confidence and energy. The choir has established a unique community with shared goals, centred around an unobtainable quest for perfection. Consequently choristers and families take great pride in the traditions of the choir and their artistic achievements.

> Perhaps one day they may even begin to regard me as one of their own, a Zhuhai composer.

Prior to settling in Zhuhai, I enjoyed a long international career in music education, holding positions in Kuwait and Taiwan, China, before leading music departments in several schools in the United Kingdom and the Chinese mainland. I try to balance my role as Music Director of the British Schools Foundation Choral Programme with that of composer. My works include the song-symphony *Songs of Awe and Wonder*, a symphonic poem *Koh-i-Noor*, *The Transit of Venus*, an orchestral song cycle based on Shakespeare Sonnets and Violin Concerto "Arin Mirkan". The latter was recently premiered in Germany by the Cologne New Philharmonic Orchestra and plans are currently underway to tour the work in the UK and China. *Songs of Awe and Wonder* was recorded by the Brno Philharmonic in 2011, my professional debut recording as a composer. My orchestral art song, *The Inspiration of Night*, was premiered at the Tianjin Grand Theatre in October 2012 by Sir Mark Elder and the Hallé Orchestra. Other movements from this work were subsequently performed by the Shenzhen Symphony Orchestra in the final gala concert of the Beijing Modern Music Festival and have also been performed in the USA.

Although I hold on tightly to my identity as an English composer, Zhuhai has very much become my home, a city that I love profoundly and one which I'm proud to be associated with. I hope to make a positive and lasting contribution to the cultural life of this beautiful city. As choral director, I want to make Zhuhai Classical Children's Choir a permanent part of Zhuhai's cultural DNA, much as Vienna Boys Choir is part of Vienna's. As a composer, I aspire to produce music at the highest artistic level and hope that one day the people of Zhuhai might be pleased by something I compose. Perhaps one day they may even begin to regard me as one of their own, a Zhuhai composer.

INFIN

THE TRAILBLAZER
BRIDGING THE GAP
IN THE DEEP
THE INNOVATOR
FLY HIGH

ITE
ZHUHAI

Zhuhai Meet

THE
BLUEPR

THE BLUEPRINT

the Future

INT

Hong Kong

In 1990, a newly discovered asteroid, numbered "2903", was named "Zhuhai" by the Purple Mountain Observatory (PMO) in Nanjing, China. It was the first time PMO named an asteroid after a Chinese city. In a similar manner as this astronomical object orbiting the Sun, its namesake—Zhuhai—is like a new star in the universe that was rediscovered in 1979, and has been releasing its boundless, pent-up energy non-stop ever since.

Zhuhai's progress is relentless. Grand schemes are reconfiguring the urban landscape and forever reshaping the skyline. Check out Gongbei Customs during rush hour and you'll experience the city at its most dizzying, with rivers of people pouring into long queues. Gaze out from the top of the 330m-tall Zhuhai Tower, and you'll see vast, vibrant coasts that seem to go on forever.

THE
TRAILBL

In *1979, a TV station in Hong Kong quizzed the public with a "riddle": A city on the Chinese mainland where people are served by only one traffic light, one main road and one policeman. "Zhuhai" was the answer given by the majority of the respondents. That was the year the United States recognized the People's Republic of China, and Zhuhai officially became a "city", and one year before neighboring Shenzhen became China's first Special Economic Zone (SEZ). It was also the year Deng Xiaoping—the "architect of modern China"—made his first inspection tour to southern China, which ushered Zhuhai into the country's SEZ frontline in 1980.*

That was only a year after Boeing announced the sale of 747 aircraft to various airlines in the PRC, and the beverage company Coca-Cola made public their intention to open a production plant in Shanghai, as part of the company's "comeback in China" strategy. The year 1979 was a busy one for Deng Xiaoping, and in many profound ways, a milestone in the history of not only Zhuhai but also modern China.

From Outlying Fishing Area to "Chinese Riviera"

THE TRAILBLAIZER

Not that many years ago, Zhuhai was nowhere in the geographical knowledge-base of people who could claim to have seen the world a little more than others. More well-informed people did know there was an outlying frontier village near the mouth of the Pearl River, where a labyrinth of swamps, streams, islands and mud flats made ideal habitats for fish and shrimp, but the "fragrant mountain" seemed to have little appeal as a human settlement.

Only 35 years later, that little-known fishing village was declared by the Chinese Academy of Social Sciences as "the most livable city in China" in a report released in 2014. Zhuhai is well past the days of being overshadowed by Shenzhen—located immediately north of Hong Kong—and by the neon jungle of Guangzhou. Today, Zhuhai is home to some of the most distinguished artists and craftsmen, as well as iconic historical sites, breathtaking coastal scenery of the Pearl River Delta region of China, and a dynamic, innovation-driven economy.

As with neighboring Shenzhen, the implementation of Zhuhai as an SEZ was largely due to its strategic position neighboring the Macao Special Administrative Region, a trading center similar to Shenzhen's position with Hong Kong. The city's "SEZ" status created the perfect economic conditions for increased interaction between Zhuhai and Macao and, consequently, the global market. As a result, Zhuhai is now a major city in the Pearl River Delta region. Implementation of the SEZ concept has successfully given rise to what is now a key port city, a science and education incubator, one of southern China's premier tourist destinations, and a regional hub for transportation.

While the city is located in the traditionally

Cantonese-speaking region of Guangdong Province, a significant portion of the population made up of Mandarin-speaking economic migrants originally from inland provinces is continuously intensifying this melting pot's unique cultural diversity and vitality.

Now a poster-child for rapid movement through far-reaching market-economy reforms, Zhuhai owes more than people today can imagine to Xi Zhongxun, whose help in initiating economic liberalization in southern China during his years as first provincial secretary of Guangdong province in the 1980s was absolutely crucial and, of course, to the mastermind of China's modernization, Deng Xiaoping, whose brave heart and great vision opened China to foreign investment and the global market, forging the country into one of the fastest-growing economies in the world for several generations and raising the standard of living for hundreds of millions.

In the winter of 1984, Deng Xiaoping made his second inspection tour to southern China. It was not a trip as breezy as his third one in 1992, when all the man's foresights had become reality and the SEZ drive had blossomed into what was later recognized as the crucial "leaps and bounds" period of modern China. The excitement and anxiety always involved when cutting a brave new path had been weighing on the paramount leader of the PRC but, during his stay in Zhongshan, he boldly refused to return by the same route he had come as arranged by the local reception team. "I never look back," a determined Deng explained straightforwardly. Back in the Zhuhai Hotel, Deng Xiaoping expressed his excitement and best wishes to Zhuhai in a calligraphic piece that will be forever remembered by the city and its people. On that landmark day, a legend was born.

Deng's confidence in Zhuhai led to the country's first SEZ economic boom, making 1984 the de facto starting point of the city's rebirth in all aspects of social and economic development. In the spring of 1992, Deng made his third "South China Tour", visiting Guangzhou, Shenzhen, and Zhuhai, and spending the New Year in Shanghai. On this tour, Deng made many speeches and generated large local support for his reformist platform. His well-received catchphrase, "To get rich is glorious", unleashed a wave of personal entrepreneurship that continues to drive China's economy today.

In 1992, only 13 years after it joined the nation's "city" legion, Zhuhai ranked among the country's "top 50 cities with the most outstanding comprehensive strengths".

Today, the children of the first new settlers in the city that evolved from swampy isolation into an economic powerhouse, linking the latest trends of the world in less than four decades, have grown up to become the mainstay of the city's incessant vitality. They are also the lucky beneficiaries of all the profound changes brought by the stunning farsightedness and willpower of Deng Xiaoping, who was so impressed with Singapore's economic development, greenery and housing during his visit to the country in 1978, impressions that carried over to affect his approach to the Pearl River Delta and Zhuhai, with such long-lasting and historic results.

BRIDGING THE GAP

The Rise of Guangdong-Hong Kong-Macao Greater Bay Area

*Tr*uth be told, one needs only to glance at the map to get a feel for this dazzling archipelago's importance—topographically speaking—and to ride over one of its many bridges only serves to compound the hunch that this sleepy collection of stunning fishing villages and pristine beaches is somewhat of a sleeping dragon. The island's time is coming, and the time to invest, insiders would say, is most certainly now.

To fully appreciate the huge scale and world-class nature of the "Guangdong-Hong Kong-Macao Greater Bay Area" strategy and its enormous implications, it is useful to take a quick look at the world's other "top three" bay economies, serving as a convincing analogy.

Located in the southern Kantō region of Japan and encompassing several of its most important ports, Tokyo Bay is the most populous and largest industrialized area in Japan, contributing a whopping 40% of the national GDP. New York Bay, surrounding the mouth of the Hudson River feeding into the Atlantic Ocean, and the San Francisco Bay Area, surrounding the San Francisco, San Pablo and Suisun estuaries in the northern part of California, contribute 8% and 5% respectively to the economy of the United States.

With China rising as the world's second largest economy, specialists ask the question: where is the "bay economy" of this economic powerhouse in the Orient? The newly opened Hong Kong-Zhuhai-Macao Bridge leads to a compelling answer. The ocean-crossing span further clarifies the scope and potential of the ambitious Guangdong-Hong Kong-Macao Greater Bay Area scheme, announced to the world by the Chinese Central Government in 2017 and putting Zhuhai into the limelight of the world's "bay economy arena". Such a new perspective and commitment, together with the "super bridge" waltzing on the expansive sea, promises to provide significant macro socio-economic benefits for the Greater Pearl River Delta (PRD) Region including Hong Kong.

This super bridge utterly alters the previous, long-accepted condition of the transport linkage between Hong Kong and Pearl River

The Ocean Engineer—Gaolan Port & Gaolan Port Economic Zone (GPEZ)

Upgraded to a national Economic & Technological Development Zone in 2012, GPEZ possesses the largest terminals of liquid chemicals and bulk cargos in the Pearl River Delta, and is bestowed with unique national conditions ideal for constructing a 300,000-ton terminal. As one of the main chemical industry clusters of Guangdong Province, it is becoming a world-level shipbuilding and ocean engineering equipment manufacturing base, a state-level, clean energy and petrochemical base, and a regional port logistics center.

The opening of the Guangzhou-Zhuhai Railway and Gaolan Port Expressway in 2012 further enhanced the potentials of the port in its development of a variety of harbor industries covering fine chemical engineering and new materials manufacturing, clean energy, and advanced offshore equipment manufacturing.

The sizzling vitality of the port has drawn Fortune Global 500 enterprises such as BP, SANY, Shell, Lubrizol, Solvay, Hutchison Whampoa, as well as a host of big shots including CNOOC, PetroChina, SinoChem and COSCO, making the area a potent energy field on the west bank of Pearl River.

West, which will now rely mainly on water transport and shortens the overland distance from Hong Kong to Macao and Zhuhai from 160 to 30 kilometers, reducing the journey time to within half an hour. As a result, Pearl River West now lies within the 3-hour transport network that radiates from Hong Kong as its center.

By slashing travel times between the eastern and western banks of the Pearl River Delta, less-developed parts of southern China will gain improved access to global markets through Hong Kong. In addition, Hong Kong will benefit from this project in the long term, through the enhanced flow of labor and goods between China and the rest of the world. The consensus is that the bridge will encourage deeper economic integration between Hong Kong and the Pearl River Delta Region, creating more employment opportunities and reducing carbon emissions by 1000+ tons per day. For tourists visiting the PRD region, the beautiful curve placed in between the sky and the sea increases the opportunity of visiting Macao and the western part of Guangdong by road or by rail on top of visiting Hong Kong. In this manner, the new multi-destination itineraries will definitely enhance the tourist experience in the region.

All in all, the intoxicating beauty of this new, sea-crossing "ribbon" encapsulates the infinite future of a city whose time has come.

DRAGON O[N]

Hong Kong - Zhuha[i]

> Earth has not anything to show more fair:
> Dull would he be of soul who could pass by
> A sight so touching in its majesty:
> This City now doth like a garment wear
>
> The beauty of the morning: silent, bare,
> Ships, towers, domes, theatres, and temples lie
> Open unto the fields, and to the sky,
> All bright and glittering in the smokeless air.
>
> Composed upon Westminster Bridge by William Wordsworth

Considering New York City's glamorous Grand Central Station with its iconic main hall, paired with the Statue of Liberty nearby, and London's gothic St Pancras Station, originally opened in 1868 and dubbed the "cathedral of the railways", what does Zhuhai's recently unveiled sea-spanning bridge network say about the city? One thing is for sure, judging by its sheer size and architectural scope, Zhuhai is surely a city on the move; ambitious, forward thinking, and not afraid to make a statement. Even before it was completed, the futuristic bridge wouldn't have looked out of place in a Stanley Kubrick film.

IN THE SEA
HZM-Macao Bridge

The bridge-tunnel system consists of a series of three cable-stayed bridges and one undersea tunnel, as well as three artificial islands, spanning the Lingding Channel that connects Hong Kong with Macao and Zhuhai on the Pearl River Delta (PRD). The 55-kilometer, sea-crossing link is among the longest fixed-links in the world and is undoubtedly the most dazzling landmark in the Pearl River Delta area.

Construction formally kicked off in earnest on 15 December 2009. The final tunnel joint was installed on May 2, 2017, with the bridge formally declared completed two months later, and unveiled to traffic on October 24, 2018.

The concept of the project is similar to that of the Chesapeake Bay Bridge Tunnel in Virginia, United States and the Øresund Bridge between Denmark and Sweden, with a 6.75km undersea tunnel allowing large container vessels to pass.

Providing a direct link for passengers and freight traffic heading for the western part of the PRD, the bridge helps alleviate the heavy traffic congestion at the Hong Kong-Shenzhen Exit and Entry Inspection facilities and reduces the economic losses arising from the daily hold-up at these crossings.

The ocean-crossing span promises to add power to the Guangdong-Hong Kong-Macao Greater Bay Area to give full play to its unique resources of ports, tourism attractions and fishing industry. Moreover, the line is, architecturally speaking, a highly impressive set of works displaying wondrous engineering prowess.

BRIDGING THE GAP

IN THE DEEP

<u>Zhuhai's Role in the Belt and Road Enhanced by CLAC Expo and China-Israel Investment Summit</u>

The proud maritime tradition of Zhuhai has put the city in a prominent position in the Belt and Road endeavors. The city's unique advantages in communicating with the outside world were already firmly established by the late years of the Ming Dynasty (1368-1644), when present-day Zhuhai-Macao region was already a significant East-West cultural exchange and trading post— at a time when China's dominance of the world's maritime trade-routes were quickly being lost to the Europeans in their hungry pursuit of gold, silver, tea, porcelain and spices. Today, Zhuhai has proven once again to be an increasingly important participant in the country's "marine renaissance". The 21st century has seen the city embracing the sea with lofty aspirations.

The 4th China-Israel Investment Summit (2018), Zhuhai

The 12th China-LAC Business Summit, held in Zhuhai, on November 1-3, 2018

The year 2017 saw the success of the first CLAC Expo, hosted in Hengqin, Zhuhai. A delegation of media representatives from the Maritime Silk Road countries took part in a series of activities to report the highlights of achievements and broadcast to a world audience the infinite possibilities of international cooperation in the Belt and Road context.

In July 2018, some 5,800 participants representing more than 2,400 companies from China and Israel got together again in Zhuhai to brainstorm about intensifying communication in technology, innovation and investment.

Jointly established by the Ministry of Science and Technology of China, the Ministry of Economy of Israel, the Embassy of Israel in Beijing and the Infinity Group in 2016, the China-Israel Investment Summit has been held in Beijing and Tel Aviv, with the two most recent events hosted by Zhuhai in 2017 and 2018.

Zhuhai is part of the Pearl River Delta, ranking among the biggest, most highly concentrated, built-up areas in the world, encompassing Guangzhou, Shenzhen, Foshan, Dongguan, Zhongshan, Zhuhai, Jiangmen, Zhaoqing, and Huizhou, as well as Hong Kong and Macao Special Administrative Zones.

The islands within the Zhuhai territory include a number of near-shore islands, often connected to the mainland by bridges or causeways (such as Hengqin, Qi'ao, and Yeli islands), as well as certain islands in the open South China Sea (the Wanshan Archipelago). Some of the latter are actually geographically closer to Hong Kong than to the Zhuhai mainland. Such an outstanding geographic location, together with a wide range of supporting infrastructure and deep-water ports, serves as a major attraction for foreign capital.

The unremitting innovation that is ongoing at the Gaolan Port and China (GDFTZ) Hengqin further enhances the city's strengths in its involvement in the renaissance of the Maritime Silk Road. The brave heart of a young Yung Wing (born in Zhuhai and the first Chinese student to graduate from an American university) is still beating in the subconscious of all Zhuhai people bracing up to develop this corridor on the sea.

In *vigorated by the power of the ocean, Zhuhai is utilizing its unique location to usher in a new wave of innovation. Pioneers in shipbuilding, transportation and manufacturing, the people of Zhuhai are using their historical know-how to sail into unknown territory.*

The city's passion for innovation is best illustrated by the swirling speed of the development of the Hengqin New Area, officially established in 2009. The hospitable array of artists, intellectuals, and business-owners, who call this promising land home, are happy to open their doors to welcome locals and strangers alike to experience their outstanding work.

Hengqin will reap the benefits of this innovative push by the Hong Kong-Macao-Zhuhai region as a whole, but will also aim to lead in a range of fields.

Hengqin's economical potential is unparalleled, a view shared not only by all people in Zhuhai but by

THE INNOVATOR

Hengqin New Area

current Chinese President Xi Jinping, who visited Hengqin four times (most recently, on October 22, 2018, for the grand opening of the Hong Kong-Zhuhai-Macao Bridge) and spread the word about the central government's "Hengqin plan" during his visit in Macao in 2009. Such a plan is part of an even larger dream dubbed the Chinese Dream, which, it is hoped, will turn into reality as the 21st century progresses. China wishes to open itself up to the world via its coastal regions, and nowhere is this more evident than in a place like Hengqin.

Today, travelers enjoy 24/7 services from the Exit and Entry Inspection facilities at the Hengqin Port. The service hours extension, starting December 18, 2014 in celebration of the 15th anniversary of the returning of Macao, has turned this crossing into a sleepless thoroughfare and changed the life of numerous commuters and visitors, who now can easily cross over for a late-night snack in Hengqin when the mood strikes them.

The 330-m tall Zhuhai Tower in Shizimen Central Business District is currently the tallest building in Zhuhai.

Adjacent to Taipa and Coloane of Macao with the Shizimen Waterway in between, and connected to Macao's Cotai via the Lotus Bridge, Hengqin was formerly made up, Xiaohengqin (meaning "Lesser Hengqin") and Dahengqin, (meaning "Greater Hengqin"), running east-west. The Chinese name "横琴" is a graphic description of the landform that, viewed from a map, resembles two "*qin*"—ancient Chinese musical, stringed instruments, sometimes referred to as lutes or dulcimers.

The two islands were later connected as a result of land reclamation and the completion of two causeways, and the largest island in Zhuhai was born, being roughly three times the size of Macao. However, in the year that Zhuhai officially became a "city", the island hosted a fishing population of only 2,000 or so people who managed a livelihood by toiling at the oyster farms spread all over the southern sections of the island. The island remained a sparsely-populated, forgotten place throughout the city's "SEZ" boom from 1979 to 2009.

Just like the chemistry between Boya and Ziqi (the most famous "qin" player in ancient China and the truest and most empathic of listeners; the classic Chinese exemplification of friendship), 2,000 years after the famous meeting of these sympathetic hearts, expressed in the melody of *High Mountains and Flowing Waters*, the day finally came for kindred spirits to reunite.

In 2009, a treasure trove was rediscovered, which is now being carefully developed to its greatest potential. Since then, the serene seascape has been ever changing— the view no longer only quiet broad bays, sandy beaches, strangely shaped jagged rocks, bobbing junks and fishing boats.

The local government's plan for this awe-inspiring island is to transform it into a piloting site for a revolutionary new "Guangdong-Hong Kong-Macao collaboration mode"

and to build a new platform to boost reform, high-tech innovation and overall industrial upgrading on the west bank of the Pearl River Delta.

In 2015, Hengqin was declared a pilot, free-trade zone, open to the world and standing at a new starting line in its exploration of economic diversity. The overarching aim is to rediscover the island's hidden gems, to invest and build up its infrastructure, and to turn the region into a powerhouse of eco-friendly business, tourism and culture.

Hengqin now hosts a string of highly innovative platforms highlighted by the Guangdong-Macao Traditional Chinese Medicine Technology Industrial Park, which was surveyed by Chinese President Xi Jinping during his fourth visit to Hengqin, Hengqin International Intellectual Property Rights Exchange Center, and Inno Valley HQ, an exciting entrepreneurial base that has drawn a steady flow of new ideas from aspiring start-ups. The resulting atmosphere of all this heady investment and growth is like a symphony being played by the island itself, constantly building in richness and intensity.

The ambitious developments have swept everyone into a whirlpool of excitement.

Progress, growth and harmony don't need to be mutually exclusive. There is consensus that such speedy growth and development will not come at the expense of the area's natural beauty and fragile ecological system—two things that help to make Hengqin a place of charming natural beauty, interplaying with a brisk, low-carbon, innovation-driven industrial scene.

Hengqin's big heart appears to be eclipsed only by its even bigger future. One thing is for sure: This big heart can lead everyone towards a future that's as close as Macao, a city that casts its rays over the crescent water of the South China Sea and the Lotus Bridge before anywhere else in China. Hengqin is making waves, and the effects can be felt across the region. The sky, it seems, is the only limit for this blessed land—and it's a cobalt blue one at that.

Hengqin Campus, University of Macao

Facing the Cotai area, the new campus of the University of Macao is roughly 20 times the size of its home campus, and is the first of many possible projects being considered by the government of Macao to be launched in Hengqin. With Macao law to be applied within the new campus, the project would also be a beautiful presentation of Hengqin as "an SEZ inside an SEZ".

THE INNOVATOR

Chimelong International Ocean Resort, Hengqin

With an initial investment of 20 billion yuan and based in the island's Southern Tourist Zone, Chimelong Resort is a world-class tourism brand launched in 2014 and run by Chimelong Group Co., Ltd, a conglomerate founded in 1989 that owns and operates theme parks, luxury hotels, convention centers, high-end restaurants and leisure entertainment businesses.

The Hengqin resort comprises theme parks, luxury hotels, business conferences and exhibition halls, tourism, shopping, and sports and leisure facilities.

The Chimelong Ocean Kingdom, consisting of entertainment facilities, amusement rides, performances, high-tech experiences and animal watching as well as the dolphin-themed hotel with 1,888 guest rooms, was opened in 2014.

Zhuhai Chimelong International Ocean Resort, Hengqin

FLY HIG

Young Soong Quong, born in Longtan Village in present-day Doumen in Zhuhai, uprooted the family to eke out a new life in America, after the family had lost almost everything in helping to finance the Taiping Rebellion. Young resumed his patriotic passion in San Francisco, where he joined the Chinese Revolutionary League led by Sun Yat-sen and worked with the local Chinese community to raise funds to support the operation of Curtiss Flying School, the school that produced China's first well-trained pilots. A man's entrepreneurial aspiration and fervent patriotic enthusiasm fostered a strong "genetic base" for aviation that is now bearing magnificent fruit in Jinwan, only 20 kilometers from the home village of Young Soong Quong—the seedbed of the city's "flying dream". The region's bright future ahead as part of the city's—and the nation's—"blue industrial drive", is unstoppable.

GH

The Sky Is Not the Limit for Zhuhai

A CITY ON WINGS

Zhuhai Aviation Town: Designed for the Future

If Zhuhai is a stealth aircraft, Jinwan is its "left wing". Hengqin and the city's Xiangzhou District sit on the "right wing". Driving from the Zhuhai Airport toward the city's bustling downtown along a 16-kilometer stretch of coconut forests provides yet another good look at Zhuhai's burgeoning spirit and unrivalled pride. After a decade of rigorous development based on solidarity, diligence and courage, the 99-square-kilometer Aviation Industrial Park (located south of Hubin Road on the Sanzao Peninsula), placed between sea and sky, has become a most beautiful "butterfly" spreading its wings and ready for take-off.

The sky, it seems, is not the limit for Zhuhai; instead, it is a new starting point.

The ground was broken in 2008.

A bird's eye view of the "aviation town" shows this vast piece of land and sea, soaked in infinite green and cobalt blue. Wuthering gusts travel northwards into the open sea. Ample rainfall forms scenic lakes of all sizes. With more than one-third of the territory dominated by mountainous area, this part of the Sanzao Peninsula presents a wonderland packed with memorable panoramas and unforgettable flora.

If "it takes one to know one", then only a true dreamer could build this "paradise for dreamers". The masterplan designer of this aviation "DreamWorks" is Liu Thai Ker, the master planner of Singapore. The Yale University graduate is noted for his influence on Singapore's urban landscape as the former chief executive officer of the Housing and Development Board (HDB) and Urban Redevelopment Authority (URA). Trained as an architect, Liu's keen aesthetic sense was inherited from his artist father, and it is fully demonstrated in the urban planning charm of the world's most famed "garden city", where nearly 10% of the

** Liu Thai Ker: the master planner of Singapore

land has been set aside for parks and nature reserves.

The design of Jinwan Aviation Town is a splendid implementation of this great visionary's experiences in incorporating infrastructure into long-term urban planning and in macro-micro balancing. In Liu's design, there seems to be a magic wand guiding every drop of rainwater and gust of sea wind toward its rightful place. Jinwan is designed for the future in the true sense of the word. In this ambitious plan, the town will rise as a "Sci-Fi" satellite city fused into the native soil and water in a beautifully scientific and perfectly natural way.

Here, the 100,000-square-kilometer Jinshan Park vividly illustrates how Jinwan is built as a "sponge city", a concept that was introduced into China only a few years ago to tackle urban waterlogging. The park's high-level infrastructural base ensures a remarkable rate of rainwater permeability, with an elaborately designed sewer system, draining the water quickly and guiding it to well-designed collection facilities for recycling. When the ground temperature reaches the ceiling level, the water in the collection facilities will be automatically directed back to the road for a cooling effect. In fact, in Liu's blueprint, about half of the aviation town will be functioning based on such eco-friendly mechanisms.

`Jinwan is designed for the future in the true sense of the word.`

Dame Zaha Mohammad Hadid

The town's iconic Citizens' Art Center, located in the heart of an artificial lake and hosting a range of world-class facilities (a theater, a concert hall, a science and technology museum, and an art museum), is a masterpiece by Iraqi-British architect Zaha Hadid**, the first woman to receive the Pritzker Architecture Prize, in 2004. On the southern coast of China, the "Queen of the curve", who "liberated architectural geometry, giving it a whole new expressive identity", released her maverick genius to her heart's content. Above the cobalt-blue lake, four golden "wings" are swirling and flowing gorgeously. The spectacular view of architectural geometry, dancing with the stunts of aerobatic pilots, seems to be close enough to touch.

** Dame Zaha Mohammad Hadid (1950-2016) received the UK's most prestigious architectural award, the Stirling Prize, in 2010 and 2011. In 2012, she was made a Dame by Elizabeth II for services to architecture, and in 2015 she became the first and only woman to be awarded the Royal Gold Medal from the Royal Institute of British Architects. She was described by *The Guardian* of London as the "Queen of the curve", who "liberated architectural geometry, giving it a whole new expressive identity." Her major works include the aquatic centre for the London 2012 Olympics, Michigan State University's Broad Art Museum in the US, and the Guangzhou Opera House in China. Some of her designs have been presented awards posthumously, including the statuette for the 2017 Brit Awards, and several of her buildings were still under construction at the time of her death, including the Al Wakrah Stadium in Qatar, a venue for the 2022 FIFA World Cup.

Reaping the benefits of the innovative push by the ambitious "Greater Bay Area" strategy, Jinwan is making waves, and the effects can be felt across the region. A full-fledged aviation industrial chain serving professionals, amateurs and airplane model fans is taking shape in this "futuristic", skyward oriented town.

The sky, it seems, is not the limit for Zhuhai; instead, it is a new starting point.

A CITY ON WINGS

The town's iconic Citizens' Art Center

AG600
A Flying Boat

"*From sunrise to sunset, humans sowed seeds, watered plants, plucked weeds from the ground and led sheep to prime pastures. It was a revolution in the way humans lived—the Agricultural Revolution,*" Professor Yuval Noah Harari wrote in his "*Sapiens: A Brief History of Humankind*". "*Eventually, people were so smart that they were able to decipher nature's secrets, enabling them to tame sheep and cultivate wheat. As soon as this happened, they cheerfully abandoned the grueling, dangerous, and often spartan life of hunter-gatherers, settling down to enjoy the pleasant, satiated life of farmers.*"

From an anthropological point of view, the history of humankind changed again irreversibly when the first boat was released into the sea and the first plane took off into the sky. Whether it was humans who tamed the ocean and the sky or the other way around, it is an indisputable fact that it is the sea and sky that turned humans into a new sort of "hunter-gatherer", sending them on to an extremely competitive "road of no return".

Humans have always wanted to fly like birds but, as soon as they actually could, it became an important part of imperial visions and a big secret to success for any ambitious nation. Historically speaking, it may have been a mindset too firmly entrenched in the "land" that brought China such challenges in recent centuries. In this sense, the country's "marine renaissance" strategy and movement toward "big planes", combined with the epoch-making Belt and Road initiative, mark a fundamental step in China's demonstration of a growing role in the increasingly ocean-and-sky-bound global network of today's world.

For a prolonged period of time, only the U.S., Russia and four European countries could make large aircraft, with the market dominated by America's Boeing and Europe's Airbus. The ice was broken by the success of the maiden flight of the Xi'an Y-20** ("transport-20") - a large military transport aircraft developed by Xi'an Aircraft Industrial Corporation in 2013.

C919**—a narrow-body twinjet airliner developed by Chinese aerospace manufacturer Comac, rolled out in 2015 and first flew on 5

** Xi'an Y-20   The official codename "Kunpeng" is inspired by the mythical bird that could fly for thousands of miles described in the ancient Chinese Taoist classic, Zhuangzi. However, within the Chinese aviation industry itself, the aircraft is more commonly known by its nickname, Chubby Girl, because of its wide fuselage in comparison to other Chinese aircraft previously developed in China. The Y-20 uses components made of composite materials. The composites are produced in China, whereas in the past they had to be imported. Certain parts of the wing such as the triple-slotted trailing-edge flaps were developed by the Ukrainian Antonov Design Bureau. The Y-20 is the first cargo aircraft to use 3D printing technology to speed up its development and to lower its manufacturing cost.

COMAC-C919 is planned to enter commercial service in 2021 with China Eastern Airlines. It is intended to compete primarily with the Boeing 737 MAX and Airbus A320neo.

May 2017.

December 24, 2017 saw the sensational debut of the AVIC AG600, code named Kunlong, in Zhuhai. Its maiden flight was made from the runway of Zhuhai (Jinwan) Airport. The last of China's three state-approved "big plane projects" and designed by the Aviation Industry Corporation of China (AVIC), it is an amphibious aircraft having the hull of a flying boat for waterborne operations along with a wheeled retractable undercarriage for alighting on land. It is one of the world's largest amphibious aircrafts, after the Beriev A-40, and is the largest currently flying, intended for both civil and military roles. In civil use, as an aerial firefighter it will be capable of dropping 12 tonnes of water, while in search and rescue operations it will accommodate up to 50 passengers. The prototype AG600, built by CAIGA, has a wingspan of 38.8 meters (127 ft) and is powered by four turboprop engines. The type of engine is WJ-6, a modified Chinese-made version of the Soviet Union's Ivchenko AI-20 series.

Airshow China

I Believe I C

INFINITE ZHUHAI

Zhuhai is the proud, permanent host of China's only air show, held biennially in early November of even years, in the city's Aviation Town—the embodiment of the future of the city's ambitious "journey to the West". When the first spell of autumn chill sets in the northern parts of the country, the sky of Zhuhai is drenched in cool breezes and braces for a gathering of a world audience casting their gaze upon the deep blue horizon and sharing one same belief. For the gravity-bound humans, perhaps the most beautiful joy possible comes at the moment of looking up into the sky and knowing that "I can fly".

I BELIEVE I CAN FLY

China International Aviation & Aerospace Exhibition, also known as Airshow China or Zhuhai Airshow, is the largest air show on the Chinese mainland, with the China International Aviation Exhibition Center serving as the main venue of the grand show.

With a reputation ranking together with the world's top four air shows: the Paris Air Show, UK's Farnborough Air Show, MAKS held at Zhukovsky International Airport, and Singapore Airshow, the Zhuhai airshow is an important event for the Chinese aviation industry. After its humble debut in 1996, the show soon became a marketplace where Chinese aerospace companies could negotiate export contracts and the country's air carriers could make foreign contacts.

Tracing its history back to 1996, the airshow grew quickly into a large trade fair, demonstrating military and civilian aircraft. Today, it is attended by many military

forces and major aircraft manufacturers, often announcing major aircraft sales. The show starts with three days reserved for professional interaction and is then opened to the general public for the following days.

The first Airshow China was held from 5 November to 10 November 1996. Performances included: Su-27 cobra, Il-78 aerial refueling, British "Golden Dream" aerobatic team and the "World Aerobatics Grand Prix". The sixth Airshow China marked the event's rise into the world's first-tier airshow "club", drawing a professional turnout of over 30 countries and some 600 aviation companies. Highlights included the Russian Knights and the British "Golden Dream" aerobatic teams. The show has since been a main international reference of the aeronautical sector.

The 2018 event started on November 6 and closed on the 11th.

II

GONGBEI

YUNG WING

AN ODE TO THE RIGHTEOUS AND THE HEROIC

THE MULTI-TALENTED MR. TONG

A CHINESE GIANT IN HAWAII

THE LONE WILD GOOSE

THE GAP ROCK LIGHTHOUSE

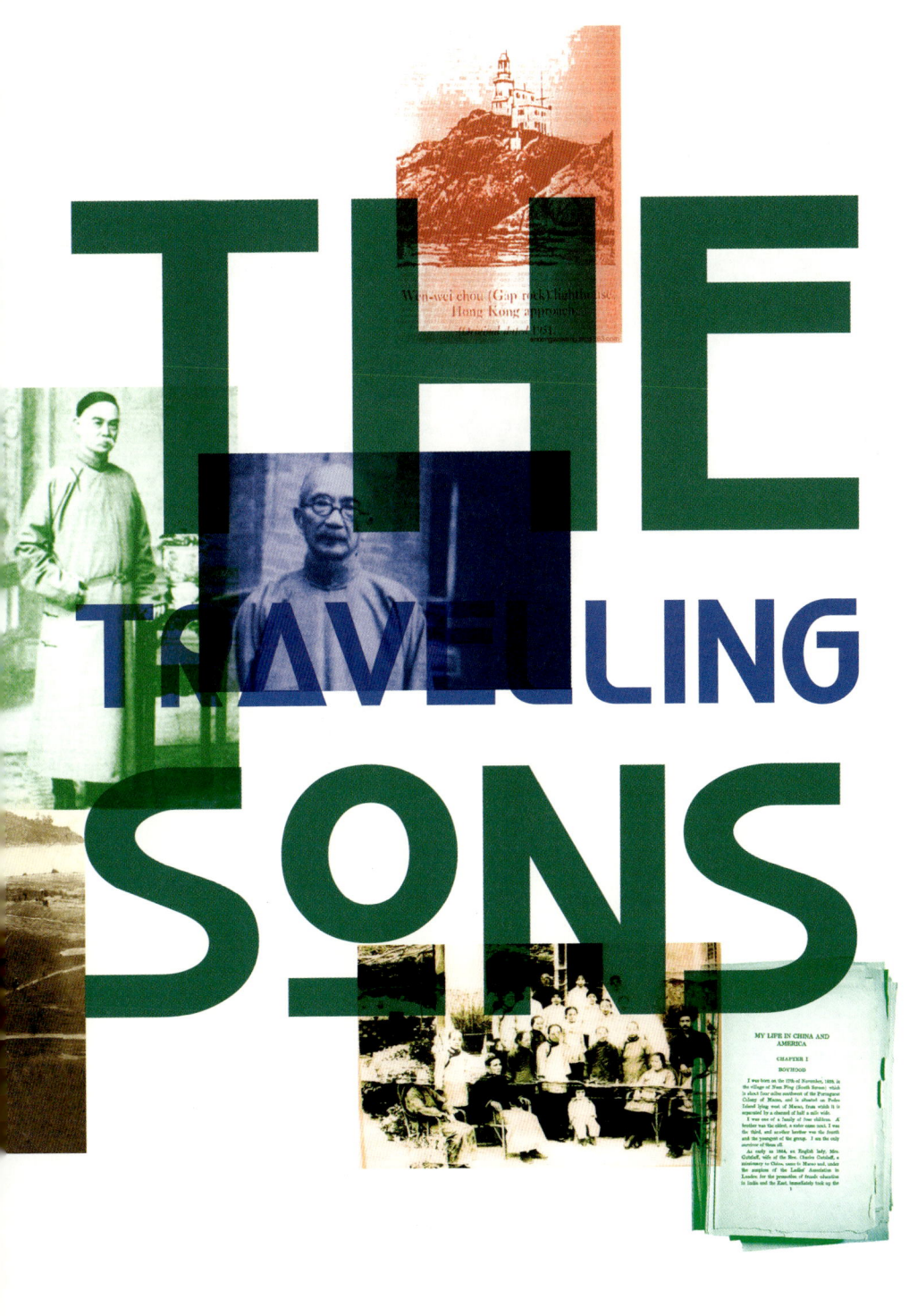

THE TRAVELING SONS

SINCE 1

The Big Connection w

拱北前世今生

GONG

Some 130 years ago, a Hungarian known vaguely as Farago landed in today's Gongbei, Zhuhai as Director of Taxation in charge of two tax agencies and three anti-smuggling divisions. Biographical information of the man may always remain sketchy, but the early identification of Gongbei, its indispensable connection with Macao, and the need to vigilantly guard this conduit to the Chinese mainland existed long before the arrival of our mysterious taxman. The concentrated potency of the little island actually started to develop three centuries earlier.

GONGBEI——THE BIG CONNECTION WITH THE LITTLE ISLAND

If the southeast edge of Zhuhai is an archer's bow and its adjoining Macao is an arrow, then the Gongbei area is the arrow's head, and the Gongbei Port of Exit and Entry is the nock. The most vital land route linking the Chinese mainland with Macao, Gongbei is justifiably called the "Southern Gate" for the reform and opening-up of China, and a point at which China's "two systems" magically blend together. This is a vivid illustration of China's wonderful practice of the principal of "one country, two systems".

688

SLEEPL

Located in the Gongbei Subdistrict in the southeastern part of Zhuhai, the Gongbei Port of Exit and Entry is one of four means of entry on land between the Chinese mainland and Macao. The counterpart in Macao, through which travelers must pass before reaching or after departing from Gongbei, is the Portas do Cerco.

Covering approximately 10 square kilometers, the heavily-used Exit and Entry Inspection facilities strewn with fancy hotels, restaurants of all culinary styles, and malls have been the busiest urban zone of Zhuhai, handling an average of 360,000 travelers/journeys daily in 2018. To say this compact piece of land overwhelms the uninitiated visitor is an understatement. The year 2018 saw a record-breaking 134 million people cross the port that has been ranking first in China for seven consecutive years, in terms of capacity to handle travelers.

This intense location makes the bustling area a hub of not only transportation and commerce but also cultural communication between Zhuhai and Macao; and for the locals this sleepless zone has long served as an ideal meeting place. Step out of this port of entry into a mind-blowing spectacle of neon at some point of the day, and you'll find yourself in "the tale of two cities" of your dreams. Most places worth visiting are conveniently close to the heart of the port area. CR Vanguard Department Store (currently closed for renovation) and Lianhua Shopping Street are two of the essential destinations for tourists. Any well-informed traveler would never leave Zhuhai without surveying the Yingbin Road, the Love Promenade and the Zhuhai Port Plaza, and sampling the smorgasbord of fabulous urban amenities that the area has to offer. The vibrant city life of the former Portuguese colony at the doorstep and mushrooming, stylish residential quarters present a fascinating urban scene, complete with an intriguing smear of historical flavors from old-fashioned architecture and the Cantonese-Macanese lifestyle, and a solid infrastructural foundation that makes the thrill of "exit and entry" a routine and convenient enjoyment for people in Zhuhai and Macao.

The port area has also been an investment haven, drawing in famous figures and business magnates for their share of the pie. The refurbishment of a string of facilities over the past decade greatly improved conditions for the everyday life of the locals and traveling experiences of tourists, spawning a brand new hub for capital and information flow.

Throughout its 130-year history of change and challenge, Gongbei has always been ready to adapt to changing conditions. One of the port's goals set for the new "bridge era" is to explore new possibilities and innovations in customs management on the Hong Kong-Zhuhai-Macao Bridge, the extreme efficiency of which is absolutely essential to the phenomenal flow of people and commerce through this relatively small passage.

Keeping in mind its historical roots while embracing the future, Gongbei Port of Exit and Entry sits atop a huge reservoir of potential and burgeoning development.

THE TRAVELING SONS

Throughout its 130-year history of change and challenge, Gongbei has always been ready to adapt to changing conditions. One of the port's goals set for the new "bridge era" is to explore new possibilities and innovations in customs management on the Hong Kong-Zhuhai-Macao Bridge.

The founding of Xiangzhou Tax Division of Gongbei Port in 1909

Macao Tax Bureau of Gongbei Port

The thrill of "exit and entry" is a routine and convenient enjoyment for people in Zhuhai and Macao.

"*yanguan* spirit"

Sunday, March 13, 2011 saw a record-breaking 300,000 people pass the frontier inspection station, marking the first time Gongbei Port of Exit and Entry surpassed its counterpart in Shenzhen in the number of travelers handled. Today, travelers enjoy "19 hours / 7 days" services from the border facility. This extension, starting on December 18, 2014, turned the Gongbei Port area into a "crossing that never sleeps", made possible by the celebrated "*yanguan* spirit". The term, "*yanguan*" is actually an abbreviation for "*yanchang*" and "*tongguan*", literally interpreted simply as "extend the open hours of the Exit and Entry Inspection facility", but, coupled with "spirit", refers to the dedication, sacrifice and team work of all customs officers and support agencies to sustain such an endless and gargantuan task. Behind the mundane, 24-hour hustle and bustle, there is still an idealistic excitement of "reform, development and national construction" exuded by the daily race of early risers commuting back and forth for a better life.

GONGBEI — THE BIG CONNECTION WITH THE LITTLE ISLAND

拱北賓館 **Gongbei Hotel** Opened in 1983, the original hotel sits in a prime location in Gongbei, with Macao close enough to touch. The centerpiece of the hotel is its main building that features an enchanting traditional Chinese style reminiscent of the decadent Epang Palace built by the First Emperor of Qin.

蓮花路 **Lianhua Shopping Street** The earliest business nucleus of Zhuhai and once the city's shopping mecca, the street has long been the city's trendsetter and is nicknamed "the eye" of the southern Guangdong "pearl".

拱北地下商場 **Zhuhai Port Plaza** For those in urgent need of currency exchange before entering one of the world's largest casinos, the underground shopping mall beneath the plaza north of the port-of-entry building has an abundance of exchange sites to choose from.

Gongbei Hotel in the old times

Gongbei Port of Exit and Entry

The full-scale service of the Exit and Entry Inspection at Gongbei is available at about 250 inspection channels, 194 for self-processing (by June 30, 2018).

PREDECESSOR 16th Century - Late 17th Century

The ban on marine trade and intercourse with foreign countries was lifted during the years of Emperor Kangxi of the Qing government, and a port of entry was set up in Macao in 1688.

GONGBEI PORT OF EXIT AND ENTRY Opium War - 1887

In the chaos of the Opium War, Macao was closed off by the Portuguese colonists and became a base for opium smuggling. To combat the smuggling that was running wild there, Guangdong Customs launched two tax divisions in Gongbei Bay and the Qianshan River area. Sir Robert Hart, 1st Baronet GCMG (1835-1911), a British diplomat who served as the second Inspector-General of China's Imperial Maritime Custom Service (IMCS) from 1863 to 1911, persuaded the Qing government to set up a marine customs agency in Macao. On April 2, 1887, a Hungarian known as Farago was sent to Gongbei to take over the tax divisions in Maliuzhou and Qianshan, and launch the customs agency in Macao.

REBIRTH 1949-1950

The Macao customs agency was taken over by the People's Liberation Army and moved back to the Chinese mainland, ending the history of colonial disgrace.

UPGRADES 1984

Gongbei Port of Exit and Entry geared up for a new phase of development in 1980, and was elevated by the State Council to bureau status on June 9, 1984.

GONGBEI—THE BIG CONNECTION WITH THE LITTLE ISLAND

1992
Deng Xiaoping paid an inspection visit to Zhuhai during his South China Tour in 1992.

LINKING MACAO

1991

March 28, 1991 celebrated the signing of a Memorandum, reached by Zhuhai and Macao, that finalized the details regarding linking the Yingbin Avenue in Gongbei with Macao.

AVIATION (since 1996)
The high efficiency and quality service of Gongbei Port of Exit and Entry has played a crucial role in the sensational success of the China International Aviation & Aerospace Exposition (AIRSHOW China), hosted by Zhuhai for many consecutive years.

1999
The Chinese Government resumed the exercise of sovereignty over Macao on the 20th of December in 1999. The moment of pride was inscribed into the history of Gongbei Customs, from which point the Chinese People's Liberation Army had entered Macao.

Record-breaking 2018 April 21
Gongbei Exit and Entry Inspection facility handled a record-setting 440,000 visits on April 21, 2018. The year 2018 saw a record-breaking 134 million people cross the port.

HENGQIN 2009
Zhuhai inaugurated its Hengqin New Area in 2009. The fast development of the China (Guangdong) Pilot Free Trade Zone (FTZ) Hengqin Area of Zhuhai, launched in 2015, has been mightily reinforced by the bold reform of Gongbei Port of Exit and Entry.

Yung Wing

A "Fortunate Son" and China's Study Abroad Pioneer in the Modern World

THE TRAVELING SONS

Róng
容閎
Hóng

Yung Wing (Rong Hong) 1828-1912

Born in Nanping Village in today's Nanping Town, Zhuhai, Yung Wing is the first Chinese student to graduate from an American university (Yale College in 1854). An early and influential figure in building business and many other relationships between China and the United States, he brought students from China to study in the United States on the Chinese Educational Mission. Yung Wing's initiative in establishing the unprecedented Chinese Educational Commission (CEC) gave rise to the Self-Strengthening Movement in the late Qing period. He is thus widely considered a trailblazer and great thinker in the modernization of China. It is no exaggeration to say that it was Yung Wing, more than any other single person, who opened a closed China to the modern world.

> The good resembles the evergreen.
> The wicked resembles the flower.
> At present one is inferior to the others.
> There is mourning and the day when frost and snow fall,
> we only see the evergreen but not the flower.
>
> —A poem written by Yung Wing for his graduation from Yale College in 1854

It was late autumn in 1828, and the Qing Dynasty, well beyond its heyday, was entering its dramatic period of decline. At this beginning of the end for the Chinese imperial system, in a village within today's Zhuhai, the birth of the Yung family's third child, on a chilly November morning, would signal a new beginning for China as it slowly looked outward through the eyes of this child and others he influenced, and entered the modern world.

Macao, known today for gleaming casinos and luxurious hotels, was then the small but prosperous center of Portuguese colonial rule, only a narrow strait away from the village of Yung Wing's birth. The proximity to Macao brought the villagers into frequent interaction with the Western missionaries and, at that cusp in cultural collision, through luck or supernatural preordination, resulted in a chance for 7-year-old Yung Wing to attend the Morrison School, established by the evangelical, Lutheran minister, Elijah C. Bridgman. The school was managed by Samuel R. Brown, a Ph.D. and Yale graduate who had arrived in Macao in 1839 to serve as headmaster of the school.

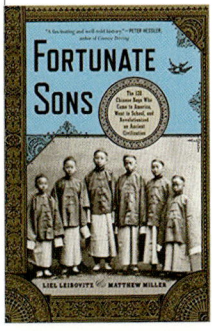

Fortunate Sons:
The 120 Chinese Boys Who Came to America, Went to School, and Revolutionized an Ancient Civilization

While his peers were struggling with the *Three-Character Classic*, at the beginning of any typical Chinese student's long journey into Confucian studies, Yung Wing spent most of his school time learning elementary arithmetic, geography, and English. The boy was so immersed in the Western curriculum that three decades later he had to call in an English-speaking tutor to improve his Chinese when he realized how clumsy he was with his mother tongue.

Yung Wing's family plot at Cedar Hill Cemetery, outside Hartford, Connecticut

A Chinese Boy's Maria Adventure

In 1842 the Morrison School relocated to Hong Kong, where Yung Wing continued to study until 1847. A year before, 18-year-old Yung Wing was surprised by a momentous proposal that Brown, who had decided to return to America due to the failing health of his wife, delivered in class: "Who wants to come along? No need to worry about tuition fees and living expenses!" At this decisive cross-road in both his life and Chinese-American understanding, Yung Wing did not hesitate and was the first to stand up, surely knowing the challenge he was accepting in being among the first to explore a whole new world, but having no way of sensing the far-reaching impact on the educational future of a nation and the inter-relationships of the world.

At a time when the imperial examinations were the absolute determiner of a young, Chinese scholar's future, studying in the West was hardly an enviable thing; the idea of leaving the Middle Kingdom and crossing the oceans to study would be seen as a wild and irresponsible fancy by the vast majority in China. In the early and mid-19th century, most Chinese people who went to America were there to labor and send home their earnings; those who had any real impact as individuals could be counted on one hand.

With the fervent missionary movement and trade activities of Americans in China in the mid-19th century as a backdrop, the unique bond between Yale and China continued to strengthen, and the case of Yung Wing shows how this relationship began to create a bi-directional flow of ideas and influence that has continued and widened to this day.

On January 1, 1847, the schoolmaster and three of his students boarded the Huntress (a cargo ship loaded with tea) departing from Whampoa (present-day Huangpu District of Guangzhou), and arrived in New York on April 12th after three long months at sea. The city of New York had a population of only 300,000 at that time, and the Transcontinental Railroad (built largely by Chinese workers), which would years later carry Chinese students in Yung Wing's Chinese Educational Mission across America, had not even been started.

Santa

One can only imagine what was whirling in the mind of this boy from Zhuhai on his first tremendous journey, over oceans and through cultures, but a process began that would transform him (and those who followed). Not losing their original culture and identity, but gaining another, and resulting in something greater than either alone, Yung Wing and later students brought back perspectives and insights to China, serving as the needed catalyst to re-enliven the ancient power, see itself anew and finally become a leader in the modern world.

Continuing their journey to New Haven, Connecticut, the boys met the president of Yale College before entering Massachusetts-based Monson Academy—the best public high school in New England, with all living expenses and tuition fees provided by the Church or other sources. The schoolmaster was recalled by Yung Wing in later years as "a man of pure character and rich experiences". It was also at Monson Academy that Yung Wing had his first taste of the "Yale Spirit".

In 1850 Yung Wing passed his exams and

Wong Foon (Huang Kuan 1829-1878): born in present-day Zhuhai, and the first Chinese person to study in Europe. He completed his medical degree at the University of Edinburgh.

Jeme Tien Yow (Zhan Tianyou 1861-1919), known as "the father of China's railroads," and one of the 120 "fortunate sons" joining the Chinese Educational Mission initiated by Yung Wing

The first delegation of Chinese Educational Mission, launched by the Qing government in 1872

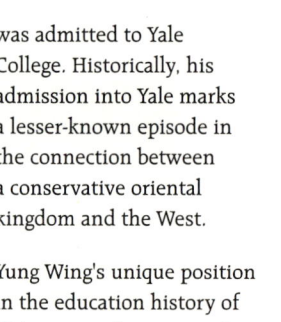

was admitted to Yale College. Historically, his admission into Yale marks a lesser-known episode in the connection between a conservative oriental kingdom and the West.

Yung Wing's unique position in the education history of China stems from not only the fact that he is the first Chinese student to graduate from an American university but the first to truly finish a full-scale program and gain a degree. One of the other two students fell sick and had to drop out. Wong Foon went to the University of Edinburgh in Scotland in 1850 through the financial support of the Edinburgh Medical Missionary Society and completed his studies

in medicine in 1855. The Church offered to lend Yung Wing a helping hand on condition that he go back to China to take a mission there after graduation, but he declined the offer, which would have ensured a secure and comfortable career pathway, stating "I wanted the utmost freedom of action to avail myself of every opportunity to do the greatest good for China."

Subsequently, Yung Wing chose an ambitious path for his time at Yale, trying, it would seem, to absorb as much of the "Yale Spirit" as possible. He was a member and librarian of Brothers in Unity, a prominent Yale student literary society, a member of the choir and the Boat Club, played football, and won academic prizes for

Monson Academy in Massachusetts, the best public high school in New England in Yung Wing's time

English competition. In 1851, at the end of his freshman year, Yung Wing wrote to Albert Booth, a fellow alumnus of Munson Academy to ask for help in acquiring study materials and stated, "Now you know probably the many disadvantages in which I labor aside from these additional studies."

In 1854 Yung Wing graduated from what was then Yale College with a BA in literature and as one of the most successful students of that year, becoming the first Chinese to receive higher education in the United States. In his autobiography, *My Life in China and America*, he warmly expressed his gratitude for the generous help from Samuel R. Brown and to the other Americans who offered support throughout his four years at Yale. "We never had to worry about tuition and fees, and every month for the first two years of the program, my parents received a living allowance. I still remember the name of many of them: handsome and noble Andrew—an editor with the Hong Kong division of *China Daily*, and A.A. Riche—a businessman, and A.A. Campbell—also from Scotland, and many others who I barely knew…", Yung Wing recalled.

On November 13, 1854, having declined yet another offer that would have promised him a decent life and a promising future, Yung Wing embarked on the sailing clipper Eureka in New York to begin the adventurous 13,000 sea mile journey home, taking 154 days to reach the bustling Victoria Harbor in Hong Kong. Yung Wing came back with a dream that had far-reaching

Rich Hall, the main building of today's Monson Academy that merged with Wilbraham Academy in the 1970s

impact on China: "the rising generation of China should enjoy the same educational advantages I enjoyed, so that through Western education China might be regenerated, become enlightened and powerful." From then on, he devoted his life to saving the weak Qing Dynasty through education and industrialization.

Back in China, Yung Wing worked tirelessly to fulfill his calling as an educator and to improve relations between China and the United States. He started by working with Western missionaries as an interpreter. In 1859, he accepted an invitation to the court of the Taiping rebels in Nanjing. In 1863, Yung Wing was dispatched to the United States by the powerful administrator and reformer, Zeng Guofan, to buy machinery necessary for opening an arsenal in China capable of producing heavy weapons comparable with those of the Western powers. The arsenal later became Jiangnan Shipyard.

Inspired by and determined to share his experience at Yale with other Chinese students,

Yung persuaded the Qing government to send young Chinese to the United States to study Western science and engineering. With the government's eventual approval, won in part due to Yung Wing's exemplary service and achievements after returning, he organized what came to be known as the Chinese Educational Mission, which included 120 young Chinese students, to study in the New England region of the United States beginning in 1872. Although the program was eventually terminated in the face of opposition by diehard conservatives of the Qing government, many of these alumni of Yale returned home to become leaders, distinguishing themselves in engineering, diplomacy, and various fields within academia. These returned students included Jeme Tien Yow (Zhan Tianyou), known as "the father of China's railroads," and Tong Kwo On (Tang Guo'an), the first president of Tsinghua College, forerunner of the prestigious Tsinghua University of today.

In December 1875, Chin Lan Pin (Chen Lanbin) and Yung Wing were respectively appointed Minister Plenipotentiary and Vice-

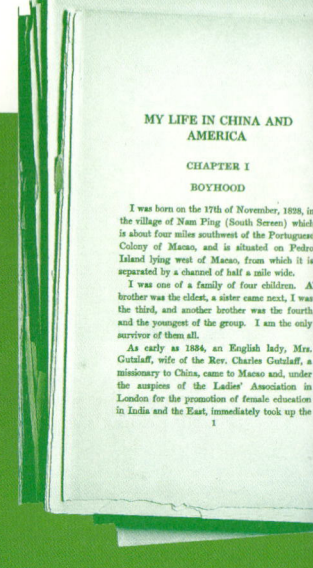

The first edition of My Life in China and America (《西學東漸記》), written by Yung Wing in 1901

The Yale-China Bond

minister Plenipotentiary to America, Spain and Peru. The year also saw Yung Wing and the 24-year-old Mary Kellogg tie the knot in matrimony.

In 1876, Yale University—the man's alma mater, awarded him an honorary doctorate in law to commend Yung for his tremendous contribution to the cultural exchange between China and America. Two years later, Yung donated more than 1,200 volumes from his collection of books that became the core of Yale's world-renowned East Asian Library. Shortly afterwards, Yale appointed the first professor of Chinese civilization in the United States. The relationship between Yale and China is both historical and intimate, and its shared vision of education can be traced back to the work of Yung Wing.

In today's Zhuhai, the man's legacy is attested to by the city's first-class educational facilities that include schools named after him.

Yale has the longest—and arguably, deepest—relationship with China of any university in the United States.

The main library building of the Yale University Library system and the centerpiece of Yale's Gothic Revival campus, Sterling Memorial Library is elaborately ornamented, featuring extensive sculpture and painting as well as hundreds of panes of stained glass created by G. Owen Bonawit. An episode of Chinese history, encapsulated in the calligraphy of Yan Zhenqing, who brought Chinese calligraphy to a new realm, is written into the wall of the entrance hall. Several tributes in the library commemorate pioneering graduates of the university. Near the Franke Family Reading Room is a statue of Yung Wing.

Peter Parker (B.A. 1831, M.D. 1834), a Yale graduate, doctor, and ordained minister, played a crucial role in the creation of the Yale-China connection. Yale's connections to China grew rapidly over the 19th and 20th centuries. Yung Wing's donation of his personal library to Yale as a gift became the basis of the Yale East Asia Library's Chinese collection, which is considered one of the major collections in the United States.

In 1901, the Yale-China Association—originally known as the Yale Foreign Missionary Society—was founded by a group of Yale graduates, and faculty members were committed to establishing a Christian missionary presence overseas. The organization still exists today and supports multiple programs focused on education, health, and the arts.

The Council of East Asian Studies at Yale University (CEAS) was created in 1961 to facilitate the training of undergraduate and graduate students, and to foster outstanding education, research and intellectual exchange about East Asia.

The university also inspired multiple generations of Chinese educators. Four of the first six presidents of Tsinghua University were Yale alumni. Today, Chinese students and scholars represent, by far, the largest group from any foreign country in residence at Yale.

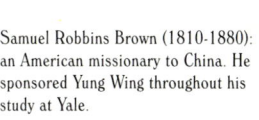

Samuel Robbins Brown (1810-1880): an American missionary to China. He sponsored Yung Wing throughout his study at Yale.

An Ode to the Righteous and the Heroic

First "Urban Planner" of Zhuhai: Tong Shao-yi

Tong Shao-yi (Tang Shaoyi) 1862-1938

Born in Xiangshan County (today's Zhongshan, Zhuhai and Macao), Tong Shao-yi was one of the first Chinese students selected for the ambitious Chinese Educational Mission and sent to the United States by the Qing government to be educated in a truly western and systematic fashion. Tong attended elementary school in Springfield, Massachusetts, and high school in Hartford, Connecticut, later studied at Queen's College, Hong Kong, and then Columbia University in New York.

The genealogical records of the Yongle years of the Ming Dynasty of China mentioned the sea area in between Tangjia Village (in today's Tangjiawan in Zhuhai) and the Lingding Ocean connecting Lantau Island in Hong Kong as "Tangzhuhai".

Giving birth to a galaxy of movers and shakers in the modern history of China, this coastal village left a brilliant mark that went far beyond the Zhuhai area. A glistening star in their "Hall of Fame" is Tong Shao-yi, whose real-life romance, adventure and indefinably charming charisma seem to out-distance any posthumous attempt at evaluation or praise.

Truly adept at both the pen and the sword, Tong Shao-yi was not completely heretical yet, on the other hand, certainly not mainstream. After turning 12, his life was a surreal drama of heroism and idealism, mapped against a life-changing cross-cultural experience in America and the stark political reality of a turbulent period in contemporary China.

Tong Shaoyi and his family, 1920

Tong Shao-yi—scholar, revolutionary, warrior and diplomat—bought a house on Route Ferguson in the Shanghai French Concession in 1937 and retired there, as fate would have it, just a year before the Japanese invaded and occupied the same city. For reasons no one will know, he insisted on staying there, as if seeking his own doom in an assassination stranger than fiction. Tong Shao-yi, a former Prime Minister of the Republic of China, was rumored to be in negotiations with the enemy, and this was sufficient to send a Kuomintang hit squad to his home pretending to be antique sellers on September 30, 1938. Pulling hatchets from precious scrolls that they brought to "present for his purchase," it was curtains for the legendary figure, who had rubbed elbows with the rich and famous and made miraculous escapes so many times before.

Born into an affluent family in Guangdong, where a new wave in education was taking shape thanks to the province's bustling foreign trade and pioneering endeavors of Yung Wing, Tong Shao-yi joined the government-sponsored Chinese Educational Mission in 1874. The ensuing seven years of cultural immersion in the United States reshaped

Built in 1932, the Spanish-style, detached garden house, located on what's hailed as the chicest street in Shanghai, was designed by renowned architect Dong Dayou. It served as the residence of Tong Shao-yi for only one year from 1937 to 1938.

Former Residence of Tang Shao-yi

Tong's world-view. Speaking fluent English, a high-spirited Tong Shao-yi felt ready and compelled to make his nation a better place. An avid advocate of American style "democracy" and "civilization", the Columbia University graduate quickly won the hearts of mainstream Americans and occasionally made headlines in the *New York Times* with his flamboyant style.

Having returned to China from his glamorous American life, Tong joined the Tianjin Tax Bureau as an interpreter, and was appointed assistant in charge of the Korean Maritime Customs in 1882. The Gapsin Coup (a failed three-day coup d'état during 1884 in Korea), witnessed the first encounter between Tong Shao-yi and Yuan Shih-kai, who was then a high official representing the Beiyang Government. A husky, red-blooded man, shouldering a gun and guarding the door, caught Yuan's eye. Both regretted not to have known each other earlier.

The tremendous bond between Yuan and Tong, like that of classic heroes in days of old, reached completion in 1894, on the very eve of war between China and Japan. Armed to the teeth, Tong Shao-yi escorted Yuan to a British warship amidst the menacing assassination conspiracy of the Japanese. Through the crisis, the two

Yuan Shih-kai's cabinet members (Tong Shao-yi on the right of the front row)

became sworn friends for life and death. This near-miss also precipitated a meteoric rise in the political life of Tong Shao-yi.

After the Sino-Japanese War, Tong was appointed Consul-General in Korea. In the winter of the year of the Boxer Uprising (1900), Tong Shao-yi aided "His Excellency" Yuan Shih-kai in the suppression of the "disturbances". In 1904, Tong was appointed Special Commissioner to Tibet. He also visited India as China's envoy to negotiate the Tibet Convention, which was subsequently completed in Beijing in April of 1906.

That year Tong was appointed Vice-President of the Board of Foreign Affairs. Shortly afterward, he was made Director-General of all railways in China. In November of the same year, he was promoted to Senior Vice-President of the Board of Communications, while continuing to serve as Vice-President of the Board of Foreign Affairs.

Realizing that his old power base was shifting during the Revolution of 1911, Yuan sent Tong to negotiate on the former's behalf in Shanghai with the revolutionary, Wu Tingfang. Perhaps sensing the approaching change in his fortunes, Tong Shao-yi lopped off his braid on the train ride south on December 8th. The result of the negotiation was not quite what Yuan expected, but recognition of the aging general, Yuan Shih-kai, as President of the Republic of China brought the public

Tong Shaoyi's diplomatic visit to America in 1908 made headlines in the U.S. media.

perception of Tong Shao-yi to a new high, leading him to the top of the "pyramid"; in 1912, Tong was elected the Republic's first Prime Minister.

The year 1912 seemed to be a happy ending and a new start, but Tong Shao-yi quickly grew disillusioned, allegedly due to Yuan's lack of respect for the rule of law, and resigned only three months after swearing in. He later took part in Sun Yat-sen's government in Guangzhou, but opposed, on constitutional grounds, Sun's taking of the "Extraordinary Presidency" and resigned from his position.

In 1921, Tong Shao-yi put aside his armor and picked up the hoe in his native town, venting all his political frustration in his private garden and enjoying his long-lost family time, planting trees, tending flowers, building bridges, and pebble trails. Back in his home

After turning 12, his life was a surreal drama of heroism and idealism against the stark political reality of a turbulent period in contemporary China.

Tong Shao-yi and Sun Yat-sen in 1912

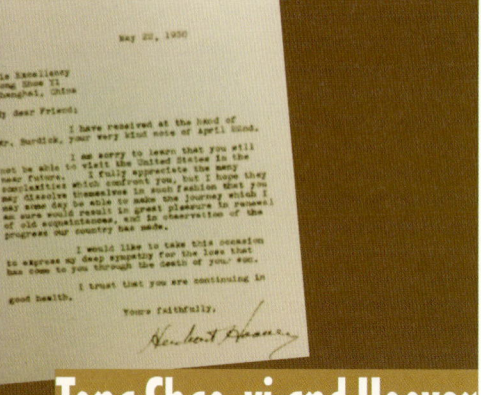

Tong Shao-yi and Hoover

V. K. Wellington Koo and Tang Baoyue, one of the daughters of Tong Shao-yi.

Tang Baoyue (1895–1918), (English name "May Tang"), one of the daughters of Tong Shao-yi, was the second wife of prominent diplomat Vi Kyuin Wellington Koo, the first and only Chinese head of state known to use a Western name publicly. Koo received his Ph.D. in international law and diplomacy from Columbia University. Their marriage took place soon after Koo's return to China in 1912. Tang Baoyue died during the 1918 flu pandemic in the US, after falling ill for only a week.

In fact, the life of Tang Baoyue was connected with Herbert Clark Hoover (1874-1964), who served as the 31st President of the United States from 1929 to 1933 during the Great Depression. The Hoovers lived in China from April 1899 until August 1900, while he worked as chief engineer for the Chinese Bureau of Mines, with his work focusing on the huge Kaiping Mines. Hoover's wife studied Mandarin Chinese and he also learned some of the language while in China. The Boxer Rebellion trapped the Hoovers in Tianjin in June 1900. For almost a month, the settlement was under fire, and both dedicated themselves to the defense of the city. During the Gengzi Incident of 1900, the wife of Tong Shao-yi and his youngest son died in a bombing. At this life-and-death moment, Hoover helped Tong save the life of his little girl from the gunfire.

village, the man who had spent most of his life riding the whirlwind rediscovered his role as a gardener and loving father. In 1924, he refused an offer to be foreign minister under warlord Duan Qirui's provisional government in Beijing.

In 1931, the former Prime Minister was sworn in as the County Magistrate of Zhongshan. That was already years after a blueprint for building Xiangshan (today's Zhongshan, Zhuhai and Macao) into an autonomous county had been drawn up jointly by him and Sun Yat-sen. The primary goal of this plan was to build a tax-free port in today's Tangjiawan, for which Tong Shao-yi racked his brain to raise funds and used his connections to spread the word. The man never had the gratification of seeing his free-port dream come true, but his determination and dedication will always be remembered by later generations of Zhuhai residents.

Tong Shaoyi's Paradise

Tong Shao-yi's lifetime fascination with plants and his brave, free soul can be savored by people today in his elaborately built, private garden, called fondly by him as the "Exquisite Yamadate", located in his ancestral hometown of Tangjiawan. Nestled at the foot of E'feng Peak on the northern side of Tangjiawan, the garden was first constructed in 1910 and renamed by Tong Shao-yi as the "Paradise" in 1921, the year he "retired from the world" into his native retreat. Tong donated the garden to his home village in 1932. Considered one of the top three private gardens in Zhuhai, it is an architectural treasure trove that reflects Tong's highly cultivated taste.

Tong King-sing (Tang Tingshu) 1832-1892

An influential figure in the national industry of China during the late Qing Dynasty, Tong King-sing was born in today's Zhuhai. He served the Chinese Maritime Customs Service as interpreter and chief secretary, later joining the Jardine Matheson Company in Tianjin in 1861.

The Multi-talented Mr. Tong

Tong King-sing

Táng Tíngshū

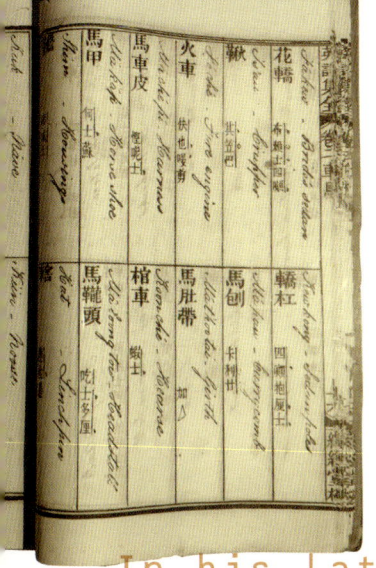

In his later years, Tong King-sing recalled his days at the Morrison School as "truly modern and elite education".

At an auction held in Shanghai in 2011, a Chinese-English dictionary with phonetic notations for Cantonese pronunciation of Chinese characters was sold at 50,000 yuan. The dictionary originally came in six volumes. The user is guided to use sets of characters that would make no sense to a Chinese reader but, pronounced together using Cantonese pronunciation, imitate words and phrases in English. For example, to approximate the word "fashion", users are directed to pronounce the characters 花臣 producing "faasan". In the same manner, "number one" would be arrived at by pronouncing 稔巴温 "nambaawan". The creator of this ingenious dictionary was Tong King-sing, whose brief but thorough education in a church school in his hometown propelled him through a stellar career that left his mark on widely ranging areas of China's industrialization. It also impressed upon him the great need for larger numbers of his countrymen to gain the ability to communicate with the foreigners in English. Although his dictionary would soon outgrow its usefulness and be replaced with more accurate ones, it perfectly fit his generation and their challenges.

T ong King-sing's death on October 7, 1892 was described by a newspaper in Shanghai as "a lasting loss for not only Chinese but also foreigners". He was eulogized by Li Hongzhang (the most powerful leader in the Self-Strengthening Movement) as "indispensible to China". During his 60 years, Tong left an indelible mark on China's first insurance company, first "made in China" railway and locomotive, first modern coal mine, first cement factory and first hospital.

Tong's father, breadwinner for the family of five children and a devoted father, made a living as a lower-level assistant at the Morrison School, working under the school headmaster Brown as the latter's footman. The school not only brought him a reliable income but opened the man's mind, making him realize the importance of getting a modern education from a "proper" school for his two sons. He ventured to talk to Brown, offering to work for him for eight years in exchange for tuition for his two boys.

In his later years, Tong recalled his days as one of the first six students of Brown at the Morrison School as "truly modern and elite education".

According to his classmate Yung Wing, Mr. Brown's Yale-style instruction brought "rapid progress in English pronunciation".

Tong King-sing was a major force behind China's first standard cargo railway built by the Chinese people. Construction of the railway finally lifted off, after bureaucratic twists and turns in Tangshan and Tianjin, on June 9, 1881, opening a brand new chapter in the railway history of modern China.

After graduation from Morrison, Tong King-sing joined his father to support the family. Although the six years at Morrison were the only formal education he had received in his life, a solid foundation was already laid for him to excel in whatever he chose to embark on later in his life. At 16, Tong joined an auction company in Hong Kong as an assistant, and soon moved up the ladder to work as an interpreter.

At 31, Tong joined the prosperous and powerful Jardine Matheson company as chief comprador, becoming justifiably the country's first in the true sense of the word and a rising star in the business circles of Shanghai. A lesser-known fact is that the prestigious "Jardine" label is behind the installation of the first elevator in China in the northern city of Tianjin.

After 10 years of working hard in that dog-eat-dog period of business and political intrigue, Tong withdrew at his peak, explaining that it was time to stop feeling "stung by conscience". In his daily races in a flashy world where foreigners thrived at the expense of the national industry of China, which seemed doomed to decline, Tong felt humiliated. He stepped down from the public stage and started a life behind closed gates, spending most of his time meditating and reading Buddhist classics.

Throughout his life, Tong King-sing had remained an avid language learner. His passion for English eventually led to the writing of China's first Chinese-English dictionary, whose six volumes covered astronomy, geography, daily life, commerce, the bureaucratic establishment and national defense.

Chun Afong (Chen Fang) 1825-1906

Born in Yeong Mui Cha (today's Meixi Village) of Qianshan Town, Chun Afong was best known as Hawaii's first Chinese millionaire, an eminent Chinese entrepreneur and China's first official representative to the Hawaiian Kingdom. Chun Afong's former, luxurious residence in Hawaii, located on the historic Waikiki Trail, is now home to the U.S. Army Hawaii Museum.

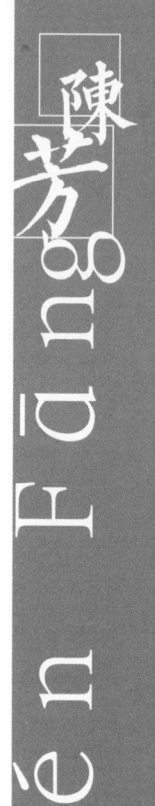

THE TRAVELING SONS

A Chinese Giant in Hawaii

C h u n   A f o n g

In June 1854, Afong and his partner leased a store from a Chinese merchant for $1,600 in Honolulu. Afong's business genius pouring into the store, it blossomed into a new business management approach that served as a model for today's supermarkets. After flames spread to the store on the evening of July 7, 1855, Afong's business was a total loss and his creditors offered to take whatever assets he had, cancel the remaining debt, and extend him new credit. Afong refused their offer, made a quick trip to China for more capital and goods and, while there, fathered a son named Lan. He was back in business within a few months.

The ballroom of Chun Afong's former residence in Meixi Village, Zhuhai

THIRTEEN DAUGHTERS

THE TRAVELING SONS

Chun Afong grew up in the bustling business atmosphere of the western banks of the Pearl River. His father, a farmer, died when Afong was fourteen. In 1849, 24-year-old Afong left his home village for Honolulu to get rich, leaving his wife to live with his mother. In 1890, the man came back, widely known as Chun Afong (misspelled by the Customs staff due to Cantonese pronunciation) and the Merchant Prince of Honolulu.

Chun Afong landed in Honolulu just as news of the California gold discovery arrived and almost every merchant and worker in Hawaii began packing for the trip to Eldorado. There were only about a hundred Chinese in the entire kingdom when Afong arrived, so it was quickly noticed when anyone took up permanent residence in Honolulu, especially when the newcomer dressed in the elegant style of a wealthy Chinese merchant. The piercing black eyes of this sparingly built man caused a stir. His first fortune, made in Hawaii as a planter and merchant, fueled his Pearl River Delta enterprises and funded his philanthropic works.

In 1857, Chun Afong became a naturalized Hawaiian citizen, a requirement for foreigners who wished to wed native Hawaiian women, and a few days later married 17-year-old Julia, Fayerweather, a granddaughter of a Hawaiian chief. Their first child, Emmeline Agatha Marie Kailimoku, was born on May 13, 1858. As for Afong's Chinese son, it was agreed

Chun Afong had two older brothers and four sisters. Fifteen of Afong's Hawaiian children lived to adulthood; and all his daughters, with the exception of Emmeline, moved to California. Afong's family life was fictionalized in a famous short story, "Chun Ah Chun", by Jack London and in a Broadway musical comedy, *Thirteen Daughters*, by Eaton Magoon Jr., a great-grandson of Afong, which played for 28 performances in 1961.

For his philanthropy Afong was granted official rank by the Qing government. Chun Afong was appointed first consul of China to Hawaii in 1881 by Emperor Guangxu (1871-1908) and succeeded in persuading King Kalakaua of Hawaii visit China in the same year.

that Julia would raise him and allow his mother to raise their first-born son in China. The result was that each boy learned about the other culture and its languages and customs so as to be prepared for major roles in his father's international business ventures.

Now a rich man, he lived in the grand style—a mansion in Macao and another in Honolulu. It was in his estate at Meixi, which included six stone mansions protected by a high wall anchored by small forts at each end, that Hubert Vos, the portraitist of the rich and famous, painted him as the wealthy mandarin he had become. For his philanthropy, Afong was granted official rank by the Qing government and, to honor him, memorials were erected in his home village of Meixi, located about nine miles north of Macao. The memorials still stand on the entrance road to the small agricultural village, but the villagers who bicycle past them today have no knowledge of the man who, a century before, commanded a business empire that stretched from the Pearl River Delta across the Pacific to San Francisco.

Chun's personal wealth was believed to be enormous and was used by him to elect Kalakaua to the Hawaiian throne and by his eldest sons to help topple the Manchus from the throne of China. His own political career in Hawaii was cut short when it was feared he would use his financial power to move Hawaii out of the American sphere and into the Chinese.

Afong left no reminiscences of his Hawaii days. For a man who lived successfully at the center of three worlds and communicated in Chinese, English, and Hawaiian, he wrote little about his life and times. Aside from official correspondence, only a handful of letters, some in English to his Hawaiian wife and others in Chinese to his business partner, survive as historical records.

Afong's former residence in Hawaii

Sū Mànshū
蘇曼殊

Gifted Polymath and Doomed Genius

The Lone Wild Goose

Su Manshu had a miserable childhood in Japan, born to a Cantonese merchant father and Japanese mother, reputedly the sister of the father's concubine, who handed him over to the fourth wife and left only three months after his birth. Exposed early on to the trauma and humiliation of being a "love child" and enjoying little family warmth in his first five years, this early experience seemed to color the rest of his life.

At the age of six, the boy was sent back to Sujiaxiang of Lixi Village in Qianshan Town, where discrimination from his father's family was added to indifference. Neglected and barely recovering from a severe illness at the age of twelve, he entered the Changshou Temple and received tonsure from a monk named Zanchu, but was subsequently thrown out for eating pigeon meat and eventually returned to Yokohama for education with a cousin when fifteen. Shortly thereafter, he fell in love with a Japanese girl but, their union being strongly opposed by the Su family, she threw herself into the sea and drowned. Re-entering the monastic life at Pujian Temple, a pattern of wild swings between the secular and sacred was established and this reputation for extreme asceticism and indulgence became one of his hallmarks.

It is, indeed, difficult to recount Manshu's many different achievements and endeavors in such a wide array. His linguistic talents brought him early acclaim, compiling the first Chinese-Sanskrit dictionary at the age of twenty-four. Residing at Lingyin Temple in Hangzhou five times between 1903 and 1917, he contributed significantly to Buddhist translation and commentary, but worked in many different languages and genres in-between, as well as becoming

Su Manshu (1884-1918)

Born as Xuanying in 1884 in Yokohama, Japan, the Chinese writer, poet, painter, revolutionist and translator left an indelible mark on contemporary China's enlightenment and New Culture Movement, not only because of his high attainments in a multitude of fields, but also for his eccentric and sorrowful character.

a revered, patriotic activist, receiving support from both Chiang Kai-shek and Sun Yat-sen. His rapacious appetite as a reader and translator would bring Byron and Shakespeare to Chinese audiences, although his translation of *Les Miserables*—the first translated rendering of Victor Hugo—was highly criticized.

It was only after the record-selling release of his collected works in 1928, a decade after his death, that tales of his revolutionary daring and hedonistic self-abandonment increasingly embellished his romantic character in the public mind. Ultimately his most remembered work, *The Lone Swan* (literally, *Story of a Solitary Wild Goose*), which was largely autobiographical, mirrored the dashed hopes and morbid emotions of a generation, romantically and beyond, and became emblematic of the Mandarin Duck and Butterfly school of Chinese literature. At the time of its release in 1912, this school was dismissed by scholars as stereotypically romantic (as the semi-sarcastic label placed upon it might suggest), but the very fact of its extreme popularity among the growing, young, urban reading public has caused it to be taken more seriously in retrospect for the insights it provides into the inner-workings of that vital sector of Revolutionary China's population.

This complex and multi-talented "comet" met his end at the age of 34 in Shanghai, reputedly from eating 40 meat dumplings to win a bet. Sadly, the reality is much more likely that he passed away in hospital after a long illness. People today can peek into the stormy lifetime story of Su Manshu at his former residence in Zhuhai's

> His rapacious appetite as a reader and translator would bring Byron and Shakespeare to Chinese audiences.

Lixi Village. How the man's troubled personality typifies the romantic ideal of the tortured writer, as well as the time he lived in, can also be savored in a cycle of highly regarded works, such as: *It Is Not A Dream* and *Burning The Sword*. In Hangzhou, if one wanders along a path on the hill-top at the back of Xiling Seal-Engravers' Society, you may view the ruins of Su Manshu's tomb among the bushes. Sun Yat-sen and other admirers facilitated the placement of his grave there, ironically not too far from another tragic romantic, Su Xiaoxiao.

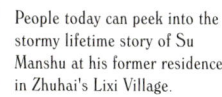

People today can peek into the stormy lifetime story of Su Manshu at his former residence in Zhuhai's Lixi Village.

The arrival of the surveyor-general— the only way of landing during construction (1890-1892).

蚊尾洲往事

THE GAP ROCK LIGHTHOUSE

An Unlikely Symbol of Enduring Cooperation

Without a human presence, a lighthouse is dead!

If you are sailing north at night toward Hong Kong, through the Dangan and Jiapeng islands, you may see a welcoming light emanating from the Gap Rock Lighthouse. If you managed to land there, you would find no hot coffee or oyster stew being offered by a lonely lighthouse keeper. Today it is fully automated, with only maintenance workers arriving occasionally by helicopter. Behind this cold, high-tech reality of today, however, lies a rich and very human history of shared risks, high hopes, and determination.

The lighthouse on Gap Rock Island, standing on China's soil throughout its tempestuous 120 years of existence, was the product of the first-ever joint venture project between the Imperial Qing government and Great Britain, helping to facilitate similar early projects in Hong Kong. It was initiated by Hong Kong's colonial government in the late 19th century, yet partly funded by the Imperial Qing government for both construction and maintenance costs. First built in 1892 and thereafter administered by the Hong Kong government until 1950, the history of this rare piece of "built heritage" embodies the collaboration between different, often fiercely competing entities at a level that was precedent-setting. The days of communication through flashing lamps, Morse code, fog horn and cannon reports are well past, along with the more romantic stereotypes of the lighthouse, but the significance of this lighthouse makes its unique history worth retelling.

> In March 1886, a Captain J P Maclear suggested that a lighthouse be built particularly for vessels coming from the south, heightening the need and, thus, reopening the proposal to erect one on Gap Rock Island.

1875 and 1876 were two big years for lighthouses in the area, with the first three lighthouses in Hong Kong opening over that short period, at Cape D' Aguilar, Green Island and Cape Collinson. Gap Rock and Waglan Islands were also recommended by Commander Reed, of which little is known, as favorable sites for lighthouses, but no agreement was reached between the Imperial Qing court and Great Britain. These two locations were within China's territory, as agreed upon by the British, so cooperation would be called for. However, the projected cost of constructing a lighthouse on the difficult topography of Gap Rock was formidable, as estimated by Mr. Henderson, Chief Engineer of the Chinese Lighthouse Department. In March 1886, a Captain J P Maclear suggested that a lighthouse be built particularly for vessels coming from the south, heightening the need and, thus, reopening the proposal to erect one on Gap Rock Island.

A number of proposals made by Hong Kong's colonial government were turned down by the Imperial Qing government until May 1888. At that time, the British Foreign Minister in Beijing was informed that the Chinese Foreign Office had authorized the construction of the lighthouse with a new diplomatic arrangement that ensured the Chinese sovereignty of Gap Rock Island and that the land would be used for the sole purpose of the lighthouse.

Surveyor General S. Brown attempted to reduce the time-frame of construction, fearing the rough seas (and lack of easy

The Foundation Stone was laid on 1 September 1890 with three blasts of whistle by "Fame".

landing area) would prevent the construction materials from being continuously transported during winter. A steam tug, named "Fame", employed from the Whampoa Dock of Hong Kong, transported all the required construction materials to the island in the summer, so that erection could be continued non-stop until completion.

Commencing in 1889, the Gap Rock Lighthouse was constructed by a Hong Kong contractor known as Tsang Keng, using brickwork for the inner structure and cladding the exterior with dressed granite blocks in order to minimize heat and glare. Flanking the light tower, the European Quarters contained a basement with storage space and a water tank, surmounted by two floors for the accommodation of the keepers. Proper lodgings were provided to ensure a healthy location with good sanitary conditions, and the

elaborate structure included a short passage connecting the European Quarters with the building where the Chinese assistant keepers and the telegraph clerk were accommodated. The lantern was 43 meters above mean sea level and was visible at a distance of approximately 32 kilometers in clear weather. No accident or even unusual incident was reported in the course of construction.

The 1st of September, 1890 saw the foundation stone laying ceremony; the Gap Rock Lighthouse first shone over the waters on April 17, 1892.

The lighthouse's extra function was providing weather information to the Hong Kong Observatory, so a direct cable had been laid to ensure effective communication. In 1895, guns were mounted to replace the fog signaling apparatus and a new magazine was constructed.

The first Senior Keeper at Gap Rock was Charles Edwin Nicholas. Typhoons and other natural threats to the island

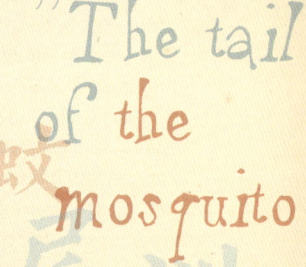

"The tail of the 蚊 mosquito 尾洲

"The Tail of the Mosquito" (蚊尾洲)

Gap Rock, a tiny islet of only 12,000 square meters, is situated at the southwestern extremity of Dangan and Jiapeng Islands, approximately 50 kilometers southwest of Hong Kong. The island consists of two main portions, with the southern strip lying in a northwest-to-southeast orientation, and the northern portion being relatively circular in shape. The top is a flat area, 23 meters above mean sea level. The island was so named because of the gap between these two portions. The name in Chinese, literally "the tail of the mosquito", is vividly suggestive of the tiny size and distinctive shape of this grassless, rocky island.

REPAIR & MAINTENANCE

In 1895, guns were mounted to replace the fog signalling apparatus and a new magazine was constructed.

were frequent. In 1893, all the glass windows of the lighthouse were damaged by a severe typhoon, raising doubts about the safety of the lighthouse. The director of the Hong Kong Observatory reported that this storm was "…one of exceptional severity at the Gap Rock and the disaster was greatly intensified by the unusual length of time the blow lasted." A consultant summoned from Britain suggested rebuilding the lighthouse on the north part of the island, but the idea was dropped due to the extremely high costs. The telegraph clerk position was withdrawn from the lighthouse staff after 1895, but two watchmen were added. In 1930, Wong Kai Chung became a Second-class Lighthouse Keeper at Gap Rock after serving as an apprentice for five years. In 1906, one of the biggest typhoons on record struck Hong Kong, once again knocking out the glass panes of the lantern and damaging the crucial lens prisms. The two derricks were also disabled and partly washed away, and the cable was broken.

With the onset of WWII, heavy bombardment and incessant gunfire caused extensive damage over the course of the Japanese occupation and civil war. At war's end, the Hong Kong government attempted to resume the Gap Rock Lighthouse, but efforts proved to be in vain. A lonely and discarded place, it wasn't until the installation of solar panels and a new helipad that the re-installation was finally done by a Chinese contractor in 1986. The lighthouse has operated on an automated system ever since, beaming out a safety-line to all. Embodied in that silent beam of light, penetrating the surrounding darkness of the sea, is a stormy episode of modern Chinese history, with both conflict and cooperation, but ending in a fashion that rightly preserves the sovereignty of China and benefits all peaceful travelers.

THE LOVE PROMENADE
AN ARCHITECTUAL COCKTAIL
THE SHELL
FISHING GIRL
DECIDEDLY SPORTY

VING

Zhuhai's pièce de

THE LOVE

A LOVING CITY

If Zhuhai were a movie, then the Love Promenade would be its star.

The gorgeous 28km seaside road may lure you to settle down in the city for good. Simply put, the seaside road is the city's pièce de résistance, embodying everything that is good about Zhuhai in one coastal belt: the city's chicest skyline? Check. Panoramic views of the surrounding oceanic seascape? Check. Trendy hillside apartment complexes and swanky-looking hotels reaching up to the azure sky as if competing for your attention? Check. Vast parklands and a maze of intriguing residential areas? Check. Winding hillside cycling trails and pathways? Check.

***Ru**mor has it that the name of the road, so straightforwardly romantic, was inspired by a loving couple taking a walk here, hand in hand. People also say that the road casts a magic spell, bringing two souls closer together. Whatever the gossip is, the winding road is indeed a place where seeds of love are sown and blossom into the city's signature social harmony.*

THE LOVE PROMENADE

No one visiting Zhuhai should leave the city without checking out the Love Promenade, created with (and married to) the city's golden coastline. A ride on this breezy stretch gives one the sensation of being outside of time; minutes and hours are rendered meaningless by its seductive maritime ambience, tropical breezes, evocative architecture, and the warm opalescence of the Zhuhai Opera House "shells".

The distilled charm of Zhuhai, this balmy, tree-lined boulevard largely traces the coastlines of the city's core urban area and is comprised of three sections. As it stands today, the 28km route stretches from the sleepless Gongbei Port in the south, all the way to the "Zhuhai Gateway" of the Beijing-Zhuhai Expressway in the north, and meanders by a dozen architectural delights, including the "Shell"—the city's number one landmark and a bona-fide architectural wonder—encompassing a string of scenic, cultural and entertainment attractions and luxurious apartment clusters served by all the amenities one would expect from a modern city.

So, be sure to reserve at least a few hours for your cruise along Zhuhai's romantic promenade. This aesthetically engineered, four–lane roadway offers the ideal means for soaking up the region's coastal charms, with the Sea-view Park on one side and memorable mountainous vistas to your other.

The silky belt can be admired from numerous angles, at different times of day or year, but most would agree that sundown is the best time to enjoy the daily spectacle of enfolding waters growing still and dark as the city gradually begins to glow and beckon.

Moving northward from the road's southern tip in Gongbei—the city's "24/7" hub of activity—one's gaze is easily lured by the waterfront panorama toward the mystical shores of the islands far beyond, until the rumble of an SUV heading deeper northward pulls you back from your daze.

Romantic sentiments aside, the road has served as the city's transportation artery for nearly three decades. Its predecessor was a 30km gritty belt once known as a "national defense highway", largely built into the hillsides by the sea. Before the construction of the first phase of today's "love highway" started in the early 1990s, the "Fishing Girl" statue had been standing in solitude on her waterfront perch for 10 years.

Although the road was intended both as a new transportation solution to link the eastern parts of the city with neighboring Zhongshan City and metropolitan Guangzhou, and as a unique solution to Fenghuang Road's transport woes, the design and construction of the Love Promenade strived to conserve the original nature and ecology as much as possible. As a result of such carefully considered urban planning, an unusually long and graceful "curve" was born. Today's Love Promenade serves as a proud testament to how well a city can be rewarded for showing respect to Mother Nature with her indigenous flora, fantastic cliffs and boulders, natural valleys and many other gifts.

Be sure to beat your own path while reveling in the romance of the modern waterfront, and check out the road's one side that blends into a myriad of historical and charming living quarters where the pathways and alleys are sizzling with authentic local life, ensuring a limitless flow of aesthetic surprises.

As a result of such carefully considered urban planning, an unusually long and graceful "curve" was born.

Xianglu Bay

Xianglu ("Incense Burner") Bay forms the visual core of the city's captivating "love curve"—embracing the "Shell", the Zhuhai Museum & Urban Planning Exhibition Hall. Here, the former glory of the Xiangzhou Port, designated briefly as a tax-free commercial port at the end of the Qing Dynasty and then continuing to serve as a key fishing center for decades, is still tangible. In the old times, it was from here that the local fisherfolk set off on regular pilgrimages to the Xianglu Cave to make offerings and seek blessings, hence the name of the bay. The hill where the cave is located cuts straight into the sea, making the bay look like a water chestnut.

The sleepy, off-white sand beach that originally was part of the bay's unique allure was restored in a campaign starting in 2015 to bring the "roots of the Xiangshan culture" back into the life of today's people of Zhuhai.

SEDUCTIVE MARITIME

CITY BALCONY

AMBIENCE

FISHING GIRL

漁女

The "Little Mermaid" of Zhuhai, a 9.9-meter-tall granite statue by renowned sculptor, Pan He, has come to constitute an important part of the city's growing identity and sense of place for residents as well as visitors when they think of Zhuhai and the "pearly sea". Depicting a fishing girl, the sculpture rises gracefully on a rock by the waterside, placed perfectly in the picturesque Xianglu Bay, harboring the "golden section" of the Love Promenade.

The folktale behind the statue describes a fairy maiden who is so struck by the local beauty that she disguises herself as a mortal fishing girl, joining in the daily chores of mending nets and searching for pearls, and doing her best to settle into life on dreamy Xianglu Bay. Eventually falling in love with a local boy who, dared on by bad influences, forces her to remove her Immortal Bracelets, this daughter of the Sea Dragon King dies immediately. Seeking the help of Jiuzhou the Elder, a life-restoring herb is found and the grateful couple, finding a huge pearl, present it to him in thanks. This, of course, is the pearl—symbol of Zhuhai—that the statue bears aloft.

AN ARCHITECTURAL COCKTAIL

Zhuhai is fast becoming an architectural laboratory. Fostered by the city's long-held importance as both a vital seaport and strategic military position, its intoxicating blend of traditional southern Chinese heritage and Western old-world charm blossomed into a mesmerizing architectural cocktail splashed all over the city and showcased in a collection of masterworks.

From buildings that look like UFOs, to gravity defying bridges that span incredible distances, the city's got the lot; and its love affair with structural wonders shows no sign of abating. Just take a walk along the city's Love Promenade and see for yourself. Better still, check out the recently opened Coast Park, where you will witness an architectural tour de force from Zhuhai's resident design geniuses.

THE SHELL
Zhuhai Opera House

A LOVING CITY

Sir Richard Rogers, winner of the 2007 Pritzker Architecture Prize, wrote of the London Eye in a book about the project: The Eye has done for London what the Eiffel Tower did for Paris, which is to give it a symbol and to let people climb above the city and look back down on it. Not just specialists or rich people, but everybody. That's the beauty of it: it is public and accessible, and it is in a great position at the heart of London.

Sir Richard Rogers' comment on the London Eye also works well with the virtual "eye of Zhuhai"—public and accessible, it is in a great position at the heart of Zhuhai and gives the city an ultramodern symbol that all can enjoy.

日 月 貝

THE SHELL

From a distance, the "Shell" looks as if a giant UFO has taken residence in the city center, and on closer inspection, the feeling remains. Undisputedly the city's main attraction—its shining light—the "Shell" is an embodiment of the city's spirit in all its neon-lit multicolored glory, with a chameleon lighting scheme that smoothly changes the color of the façade. The visual spectacle can be admired from afar, for example, while cruising down the Love Promenade or from your hotel room where you open the window and sip on iced coffee as the breeze plays with your hair.

Covering 59,000sqm of land and reaching 90 meters at its highest point, the "Shell" is a breath-taking mix of curvy lines and smooth glistening surfaces, featuring a modern expressionist, futuristic design, inspired by the city's marine quality and the formation of pearls. Due to its special location on the waterfront of an island, the opera house is designed to be able to stand up to the ravage of a category-12 typhoon and uses high-tech external wall materials with stunning anti-humidity capability.

Though the two "shells" appear uniformly glossy white from a distance, they actually feature a subtle mesh-style pattern that slightly resembles a huge spoked bicycle wheel, and at different points in the day, produces a tantalizing spectrum of creamy hues.

The Kunkel Group, known for having turned depressed areas of downtown into prominent landmarks for the residents of Evansville to enjoy for years to come, acted as a major player for the stage machinery design of the project, with the sign system design by a prestigious company from Japan and the lighting crafted by Speirs + Major (a UK lighting design practice noted for its illumination of many prominent buildings, including Barajas

Zhuhai Opera House

The Zhuhai Opera House, or the "Shell", as it is more often called, is the world's latest "opera house on the sea", the first one being the Sydney Opera House, designed by Danish architect Jorn Utzon and regarded as one of the 20th century's most famous and distinctive buildings.

International Airport, the Millennium Dome and King's Cross Central, London).

The opera house's acoustic mechanism, designed by Marshall Day, ensures a perfect audio experience for people sitting in the last row of the main concert hall that has a seating capacity of 1,550.

The design of the "Shell", inspired by Italian artist Sandro Botticelli's *The Birth of Venus*, hints at the philosophy of marine life—the kind of beauty that is crafted and perfected by the elapse of time. The birth of a pearl is a wondrous process beyond description—the seemingly motionless pregnancy is a momentum-gaining process that simply creates the most beautiful life in the world. Like the symbiotic relationship between a shell and a pearl, art and the city of Zhuhai are giving life to each other. Such an inspiring structure, and so well situated, perfectly expresses the soul and

> Such an inspiring structure, and so well situated, perfectly expresses the soul and mission of Zhuhai—a life-giving city that is making progress every day.

mission of Zhuhai—a life-giving city that is making progress every day.

The debut of the "Shell" in 2017 was also a dream come true for Ma Long, core member of the design team. Approached with the job offer while in the midst of crafting Beijing International Airport's new terminal, he took up the challenge only after a long week of consideration. "It is one of the most exciting and stirring works I've ever done in my life," the architect shared.

The structure also houses an array of amenities such as cafes, restaurants and retail outlets. The multi-venue performing art center has never ceased growing since its opening. It has been continuously enriched not only in its indoor facilities but also in its public space and surrounding areas. Mr. Ma Long predicted in regard to the project: "The opera house will subvert all the parochialism about what art really is and present its infinite possibilities." And, under the blazing sun of southern China, the translucent "shells" twinkle like the two silken wings of a dragonfly, as if ready to fly beyond the horizon, where the "infinite possibilities" of the "city of pearls" are waiting.

Zhuhai's Sporting Pedigree Put under the Microscope

DECIDEDLY
SPORTY

Feeling the urge to get moving and work up a sweat? The mercury rises, and the amount of clothing we wear concurrently plummets. Now seems like as good a time as any to hit the treadmill and shed as many of those extra winter pounds as possible.

If a real treadmill bores you, try Zhuhai and take a look at the sports the city's most colorful sportsmen and sportswomen practice. The city's brisk sports scene, based on the bestowments from the sea and the city's fun-loving and health-conscious open-air sports enthusiasts, will surely open your eyes to new and fun ways to shake a leg and get fit. Golfing, yachting, marathon, rock-climbing, car-racing, and tennis are all sports with a ready made community of participants right here in the city who are waiting for you to lace up and join in. With upstarts and established teams alike, competing in the country's top sporting leagues, the city's sporting life is rich and varied, and full of surprises for those who care to dig deep enough.

The vibrant, coastal city is decidedly sporty, drawing Stefanie Graf for its openness and growing power embodied in the WTA Elite Trophy and harnessing the glare of the world's media.

容國團
Róng Guótuán

Rong Guotuan (1937-1968)

Born in Hong Kong in 1937, with family roots from Nanping Village in present-day Zhuhai. The first world champion in the sports history of People's Republic of China, Rong Guotuan started playing table tennis at a young age and participated in competitions in Hong Kong as a junior.

In 1941, the outbreak of the Pacific War forced Rong Mianzhi to quit his maritime job in Hong Kong and take his family back to his home village in Zhuhai. The next year, he managed to enroll his six-year-old son at Zhenxian School, founded by Yung Wing, the first Chinese student to graduate from an American university, from his own pocket in 1871, as the first private school open exclusively to overseas Chinese in Guangdong Province.

GLORY ROAD

Rong Guotuan

The skinny little boy soon proved himself not only a successful student but also an all-round prodigy, releasing his athletic hormones by playing ping-pong. At that time, the fad of whacking the white celluloid ball had just been imported into China, and it did not take long for the first-grader to become the uncrowned "table tennis king" of the school.

The name of that boy is Rong Guotuan, who left an indelible mark in not only the history of China's "national sport" but also in the diplomatic glory of the nation during his lifetime.

The Rong family moved back to Hong Kong after the war, and Rong's father resumed his work on the sea, sending his son into the Salesian English School. Rong Guotuan soon had to drop out due to financial difficulties, and did not get a chance to play ping-pong again until the Hong Kong Federation of Trade Unions was restored. He joined a local ping-pong club at the age of 15, and soon rose to his fame as a top player.

In 1957, a 20-year-old Rong Guotuan, still wet behind the ears, smashed world champion Tiamura Ichiro, representing the Japanese ping-pong team that was then in its heyday, into a bloody pulp. The landslide victory brought Rong Guotuan into the limelight of the world table tennis scene, but quickly dragged him into a world of venality and dishonesty that made him sick. The man's aversion to the high-pressure business world in Hong Kong, entangled with influences from his left-leaning family tradition, eventually led to his decision to quit his Hong Kong identity. In the winter of 1957, Rong Guotuan crossed the border at the Luohu Port in Shenzhen and settled his athletic passion at the Guangzhou Institute of Physical Education.

It was a small step for a man, but a giant leap for the sportsmanship of a nation. "Today is my first day in my new life," Rong Guotuan recorded his excitement in his diary.

Rong's participation in the World Table Tennis Championships began in Dortmund, 1959. The Chinese men's team faced Hungary at the semifinals of the team competition. Rong lost to Zoltán Berczik, the 1958 European champion, in three games. He defeated Laszlo Foldy but lost to the 1953 World Championships winner Ferenc Sidó at the eighth team match.

In the men's singles competition, Rong recorded seven straight wins to clinch the men's world championship, becoming the first world championship winner after the foundation of the People's Republic of China.

The name of the first table-tennis ball made in China for international competitions, "Red Double Happiness (红双喜)", was prompted by a comment made by Premier Zhou Enlai during the celebrations of the 10th Anniversary of the PRC's establishment that same year in which he stated that there were two "happy events" that year, alluding to Rong's victory at the Championships.

At the 1961 World Table Tennis Championships in Beijing, Rong helped the Chinese men's team win the first team title by defeating Japan and Hungary in the finals. After 1964, he worked as the coach of the Chinese women's team, guiding them to win their first championship at the 1965 World Championships.

Zhang Lianwei (1965-)

Born in Nanshui Town, Zhuhai, Zhang Lianwei is the first golfer from the People's Republic of China to achieve substantial success on the international professional circuit. In January 2003 he became the first Chinese golfer to win on the European Tour, and the following year became the first to compete in the Masters Tournament, one of the four major championships in the world's golfing arena.

BORN TO GOLF

When China's first golf course opened door in Zhongshan City, Guangdong Province in 1984, the Chinese mainlanders who knew anything about "golfing" could be quickly counted, and such terminology as "the teeing ground", "fairway" and "putting green" sounded like extraterrestrial language. The next year saw a team of 10 people selected from a school in Hebei Province sent to Japan by the China Golf Association for a three-year training program and the opening of the Zhuhai International Golf Club, where China's first professional golfer rose to stardom from his humble roots.

Born in a farmer's family operating on a shoestring budget and having a worrisome world of daily difficulties to face, Zhang Lianwei joined Zhuhai Athletic Committee to specialize in javelin throwing and basketball after graduation from junior high school, with a future that looked grim. When offered a chance to choose from golf and bowling as a new professional pathway consideration, Zhang Lianwei chose the small, white ball—almost on a whim—although at that time the only thing he knew about the game was that a white ball had to be played into a hole, never guessing the decision was destined to break the ice in China's athletic pursuit in a field long-dominated by the West.

The 20-year-old started as a caddie, picking up the basics about the game at every chance and collecting tips to help his family, while making friends with the other caddies. His interest in the sport soon developed into dedication to be a serious player. Zhang's hard work and talent caught the eye of the Japanese manager of the golf club, who not only tacitly allowed the aspiring young man to use the facilities to practice putting but also later decided to become his first coach.

Only three years later, Zhang Lianwei won the China Amateur Open Championship, going on to win a total of three times before turning professional in 1994.

Early in his career, Zhang won a number of smaller tournaments around Asia, in China, Malaysia and Thailand. He has competed predominantly on the Asian Tour since 1997, and has also played extensively on the Japan Golf Tour. He won a tournament in Canada in 2000.

Zhang came to global attention at the 2003 Caltex Singapore Masters, where he edged out Ernie Els with a birdie on the final hole to become the first Chinese golfer to win on the European Tour. With this victory he also became the first Chinese golfer to make the top 100 in the Official World Golf

Rankings. As a result, in 2004 he received a special invitation to play in the Masters Tournament, becoming the first player from the Chinese mainland to compete in the tournament. His invite, however, drew significant criticism, with many players believing that there were other Asian golfers more deserving of a place in the Augusta field, but his continued excellent performance eventually overcame this skepticism.

Zhang has won a total of five tournaments on the Asian Tour. He has also won six times on the China Tour, where he topped the Order of Merit in 2006.

In 2009, while being invited to compete in the Omega European Masters in Crans-sur-Sierre, Switzerland, Zhang met Stéphane Barras, the local club pro, who later became his coach. In April 2010, Zhang regained his title at the PGA of China and, in 2011, finished 13th at the China Open, co-sanctioned by the European Tour, OneAsia tour and Asian Tour, gaining the best ranking of all Chinese participants that year.

In 2014, Zhang hit the very first tee shot in the history of the newly established PGA Tour China. In 2015 he was a rookie on the European Senior Tour, winning his first senior title, the SSE Enterprise Wales Senior Open, in 2016.

BOYS AND GIRLS

Zhuhai's New Sports Blueprint in the Making

A LOVING CITY

Sports have been well woven into the urban fabric of Zhuhai, adding fascinating color and variety to the city's charisma, ranking Zhuhai in China's first-tier of water sports and many other high-end outdoor sports events.

In 2017, the city's Culture, Sports and Tourism Bureau, working in collaboration with local sports promotion companies and schools, launched five amateur training bases, covering golf, yachting, baseball, and fencing, in order to break new ground in the promotion of juvenile sports development. It is not difficult to imagine that, in the predictable future, the children playing carelessly and sweating profusely on the playgrounds today will be the driving force of the country's new sports circuit in the future.

BE AMBITIOUS

THE ULTIMATE MATCH

A LOVING CITY

"Queen of the Lawn" in Zhuhai

When the Women's Tennis Association invited "Steffi" Graf, regarded by many to be the greatest female tennis player of all time, to take part in the organization's 40th anniversary party in 2013, she declined the invitation. That was 14 years after the "Queen of the Lawn" had retired while ranked No. 3 in the world.

However, the German, former professional tennis player was in Zhuhai three times in 2016, 2017, and 2018, displaying her stunning versatility across all playing surfaces with a spectacular show on the world's longest sea-spanning bridge and wowing fans with an exhibition match at the Zhuhai Tower, where she played with Anastasta Pavlyuchenkova at an altitude of 330 meters. At the Zhuhai Hengqin International Tennis Center, she showed her motherly, encouraging patience

22-time Grand Slam champion Stefanie Graf, as the WTA Elite Trophy Ambassador, traded groundstrokes with Russian, Anastasta Pavlyuchenkova, on a specially-constructed court atop the 330m-tall Zhuhai Tower, November 4, 2017.

holding little tennis hopefuls' hands and demonstrating footwork and her powerful forehand drive, just like her tennis-coach father had introduced his three-year-old daughter to tennis by teaching her how to swing a wooden racket in the family's living room many, many years earlier.

The accomplishments and charisma of Graf need no elaboration. Her 22 Grand Slam singles titles put her second on the list of major wins in female competition since the introduction of the Open Era in 1968. In 1988, she became the first and only tennis player (male or female) to achieve the Golden Slam by winning all four Grand Slam singles titles and the Olympic gold medal in the same calendar year. Furthermore, she is the only tennis player to have won each Grand Slam tournament at least four times.

Graf was ranked No. 1 in the world by the Women's Tennis Association (WTA) for a record 377 total weeks—the longest period for which any player, male or female, has held the number-one ranking since the WTA and the Association of Tennis Professionals began issuing rankings.

Graf's athletic ability and aggressive game, played from the baseline, have been credited with developing the modern style of play that has come to dominate today's game. She is the only singles player (male or female) to have achieved a Grand Slam since hard court was introduced as a surface at the US Open in 1978. Consequently, Graf's Grand Slam was achieved on grass, clay, and hard court while the previous five Grand Slams were decided on only grass and clay.

Along with countryman Boris Becker, Graf was considered instrumental in popularizing tennis in Germany, where it has remained a highly popular sport ever since. In 1991, the Steffi Graf Youth Tennis Center in Leipzig was dedicated. She is the founder and chairperson of "Children for Tomorrow", a non-profit foundation established in 1998 for implementing and developing projects to support children who have been traumatized by war or other crises.

Graf was inducted into the Tennis Hall of Fame in 2004.

So, the question is, what was it that brought Graf to Zhuhai, a city that is manifestly "softer" than Beijing and Wuhan?

One has good reasons to believe that Graf chose Zhuhai for some reason, something that the city and the urban-based sport share—something that touches the heartstring of the "Queen of the Lawn", who once gave the answer to

On November 3, 2018, Graf, together with China's top-ranked women tennis player Wang Qiang and Belgian player Elise Mertens, showcased their mastery of the sport in an unusual and inspired performance on the tarmac of the China Aviation Industry General Aircraft Zhuhai General Aviation R&D and Manufacturing Base (the "Base").

the question, "How do you want to be remembered?" in a press conference, as "a dedicated mother and wife". Perhaps, the openness of Zhuhai and the spotless, vast sea perfectly match the core philosophy of the blue-blooded sport; that is, elegant and dynamic, with fair play and infinite glamour. The demure, engaging smile on Graf's face and the heartfelt sincerity shown in her meeting with Chinese fans during her visit in Zhuhai already serve as a brilliant answer to the question.

"Let's share the excitement of being the witnesses of the rise of China's emerging tennis power in the country's most livable city," Graf sent her best wishes for the city on the official website of WTA.

Graf married former world No. 1 men's tennis player Andre Agassi in 2001. They have two children—Jaden Gil and Jaz Elle. Maybe the "green and blue" city in southern China reminds her of Summerlin, a community in the Las Vegas Valley, where the Graf-Agassi family resides and enjoys the company of her mother and brother, Michael Graf, with his four children.

> Perhaps, the openness of Zhuhai and the spotless, vast sea perfectly match the core philosophy of the blue-blooded sport; that is, elegant and dynamic, with fair play and infinite glamour.

Czech professional tennis player Petra Kvitová, known for her powerful left-handed groundstrokes and variety, at the 2016 WTA Elite Trophy Zhuhai.

2016 WTA Elite Trophy Zhuhai

WTA Elite Trophy Zhuhai

The second-tier, year-end professional women's tennis tournament on the WTA Tour, it is the successor event of the WTA Tournament of Champions which took place from 2009-2014. The inaugural edition was held in 2015, offering $2.15 million in prize money. Zhuhai hosts the WTA Elite Trophy for the first five years until 2019, with the Hengqin International Tennis Center serving as the venue.

The Elite Trophy takes place at the end of each season in two disciplines: singles and doubles. The singles event features 12 players (11 of them ranked from 9th to 19th on the final table of the WTA ranking, and one wildcard). The players are split into four groups of three, with the group winners advancing to the single elimination semifinals. The doubles championships feature six teams in two groups with the group winners contesting the final.

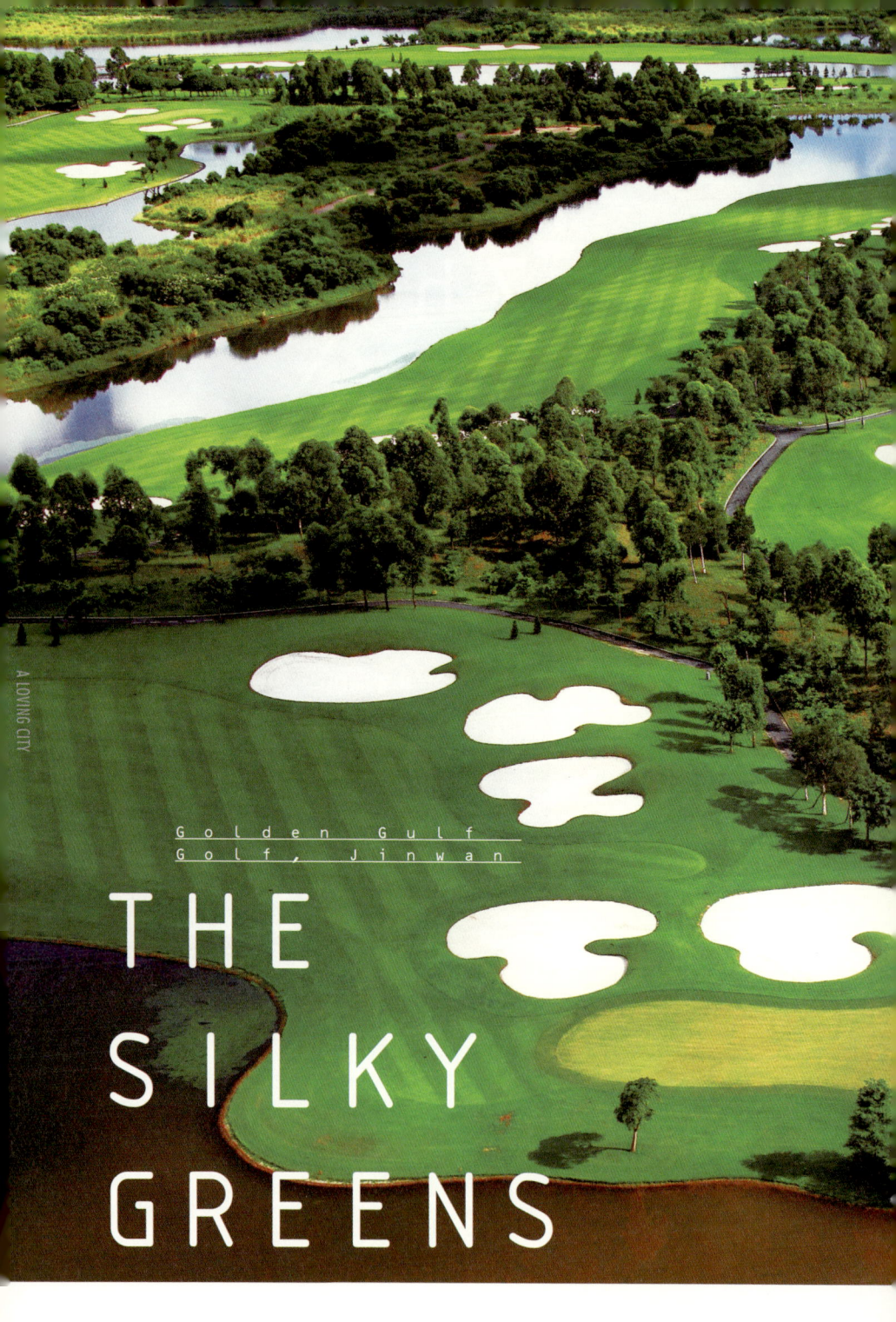

A LOVING CITY

Golden Gulf Golf, Jinwan

THE SILKY GREENS

Golden Gulf's strong Scottish flavor is crafted by Colin Montgomerie.

A LOVING CITY

Zhuhai's historical Tangjiawan area hosts the country's second golf course, laid down in 1985 to declare the city's golfing ambition. Over the past three decades, Zhuhai Golf Club witnessed the rise of China's first golf champion and the country's first golfing generation, and has grown to be the most senior in the city's golfing destinations and a prestigious resort serving golfers from all over the world. The 360-degree views from the resort's various vantage points are simply breathtaking.

The year 2003 saw the opening of Golden Gulf Golf Resort, built on 500 hectares of reclaimed land and put together by Scottish professional golfer Colin Montgomerie, in the city's "aviation town" in western Jinwan District. Golden Gulf is a mere half an hour's drive from downtown Zhuhai. Composed of an 18-hole course and a 9-hole floodlit course, the only one of its kind in Zhuhai, the high-class resort adds a splendid Scottish touch to the city's golfing panorama, creating a striking contrast to its predecessors.

The natural topography of the terrain allows Colin Montgomerie to implant early Scottish golf course design elements, or "golf links", into this fascinating seaside site. The cunning names of the course's different zones: Troon, Turnberry, Nairn, fully demonstrate the designer's wish to add flavor of his homeland to Asia. The clubhouse decor too has a very strong Scottish feel, suggestive of the designer's roots.

As the name suggests, the course is characterized by the strong presence of water. In fact a first impression would be that the course was completely surrounded by water. And yet, only three of the 27 holes in this course of bent, grass-covered fairways and Tifdwarf'ed greens require an across-the-water hit. In addition to the brilliant emerald-blue of the surrounding sea contrasting with the silky greens, it is generally a very golfer-friendly course.

Lakewood Golf Club, Zhuhai

Sited in the gorgeous Danan Mountain area in Jinding Town, Zhuhai, and crafted by J. Michael Poello, founder of JMP Golf Design Group, Lakewood Golf Club boasts a lake zone that is second to none in Zhuhai.

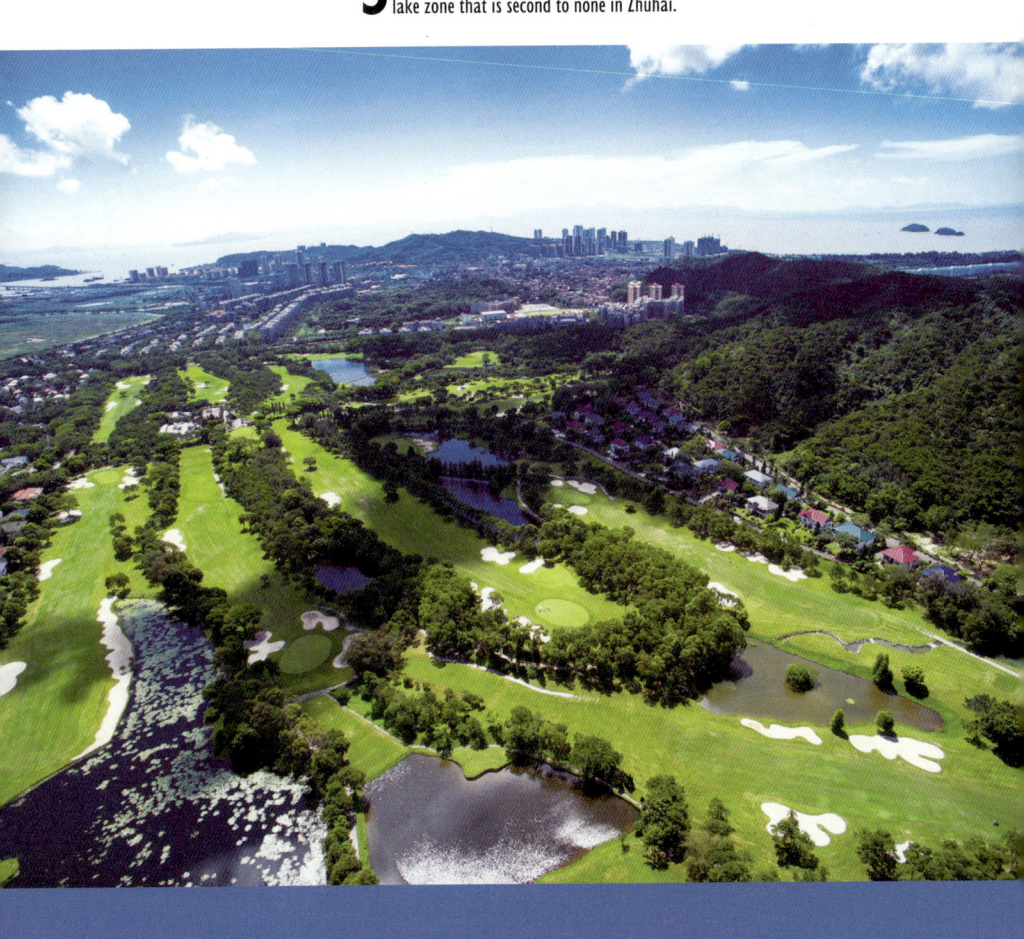

For some, life is either a daring adventure or nothing. People living in the sun-drenched "City of a Hundred Islands" are born to ride the waves. Zhuhai hosted the China Sailing Championships, ranking among the largest and most influential national competitions in China, for two consecutive years in 2016 and 2017. The year 2018 saw the success of the Jiuzhou Cup Wanshan Sailing Regatta held in the city's Wanshan Archipelago. The city's unique marine resources and winding coastlines are ideal for professional training of yachting sports and water leisure.

Zhuhai's Yachting Craze

SAIL INTO THE FUTURE

FAST & FURIOUS

Zhuhai International Circuit (ZIC)

A LOVING CITY

Located in Jinding Town, the circuit is designed by Australian company, Kinhill Engineers Pty Ltd, the same group which created the Formula One circuit in Adelaide, and is an FIA Grade II certified circuit. The original circuit contained 16 corners. Running clockwise only, the circuit is 4.3 kilometers long and has 14 turns, 9 of them being right turns, with 5 left turns. The longest straight-away is at the start/finish section, and is 900 meters long and 14 meters wide at its widest. Alexandre Imperatori, A1 Team Switzerland's rookie driver, observed that there are lots of overtaking places in the circuit because of the combination of straight-aways, hard braking areas for hairpins, and tight corners, followed by the need for rapid acceleration on the long straight-aways. A kart circuit was added to the ZIC facility in 2004.

The first international race held at the circuit was the BPR Global GT Series, with the circuit soon becoming a hotbed of local motorsports, with teams from Hong Kong and Macao setting up their bases inside the circuit garages.

The fastest qualifying lap ever at the circuit was set by a Lola-Zytek A1 Grand Prix car on the fourth round on December 16, 2007 during the 2007-08 A1 Grand Prix season, driven by Michael Ammermüller and managing a lap of 1:23.203. However, this is not considered the lap record since lap records are taken from racing laps and not qualifying. The fastest unofficial lap ever at the circuit was set by a 2007 Panoz DP01 Champ Car on November 30, 2006, driven by Roberto Moreno.

The circuit is also a prominent motorsport event organizer and promoter in China. It has organized and promoted the FIA GT Championship in China and, in 2007, signed a contract with China Motorcycle Sports

Association to promote the inaugural China Superbike Championship.

The circuit is the promoter of the China Superbike Championship, established in 2007 and sanctioned by the China Motorcycle Sports Association, CMSA.

ZIC also organizes the Circuit Hero and Circuit Hero GT race series, which allows Chinese citizens to participate. The Hong Kong Touring Car Championship and the Macao Touring Car Championship have both run the majority of their races at ZIC since they began.

AFOS has been held at the circuit many times since its inception in 1994. The 2006 Asian Festival of Speed (AFOS) drew a record 33,000 people flocking to watch the races.

The Asian Formula Three Championship and the FIM Asia Road Racing Championship races are also hosted by the circuit annually.

In May 2004, the Endurance World Championship Zhuhai 6 Hours race was held at the circuit. This was the first time an international motorcycle race was held here. In November 2004, the circuit was fully renovated and once again the FIA GT Championship was staged.

On 10 June 2010, the ACO announced that the Chinese round of the 2010 Le Mans Intercontinental Cup—The 1000 km of Zhuhai, would be held at ZIC.

On 13 November 2011, the ACO organized the 2011 6 Hours of Zhuhai at the circuit as the finale of the 2011 Intercontinental Le Mans Cup season.

Since 2005, the circuit has become a hive of track activities, with a large number of auto-related launches and events held at the circuit, as the battle for car sales in China has heated up. Auto dealers and manufacturers do their best to lure more customers by allowing them to drive freely on the track and pampering them off it.

ZIC has also been simulated on the racing simulator, Project CARS. In March 2018, the track was released for Raceroom Racing Experience.

A LOVING CITY

LEAGUE demacia cup 2018 OF

LEAGUE OF LEGENDS

LEGENDS

Zhuhai is the host of the 2018 Demacia Cup, sponsored by Tencent Games working in collaboration with MarsTV. Held at the Hengqin International Tennis Center in Zhuhai on May 31, June 3, the 2018 arena drew participation from eight top teams in China. The four-day thrill opens a new page in the city's electronic sports vista, making Zhuhai the first leg of Tencent's newly launched "City Development and Electronic Sports" campaign.

China's Maritime

Allure Distilled

It Has to be ... the Islands

There midnight's all a glimmer, and noon a purple glow,
And evening full of the linnet's wings.
I will arise and go now, for always night and day.

"The Lake Isle of Innisfree"
by William Butler Yeats

Looking for a real taste of the coasts of southern China? Yearning for the feel of leaving the land for a day or two and waking up into a world of crashing waves, golden sands, and infinite, tantalizing turquoise blue? Zhuhai, the city that boasts the longest coastline in the Pearl River Delta, has it in spades. The collection of 147 islands (covering over 500 square meters), strewn throughout the territory of this "City of a Hundred Islands" and placed in between infinite greenery and cobalt blue, makes Zhuhai a more than ideal, marine tourist destination in southern China, especially when taking into consideration the stampeding crowds in some of the other popular seaside spots.

This city's uniquely rich, island resources and coastline of nearly 700 kilometers extend far beyond what one solitary trip can offer if one truly wants to savor the region's unrivalled coastal beauty. The winding coastlines sprawl, stretch, and glaze into the sparkling horizon, creating a dreamy vista resembling a full-length shot in one of those New Wave films.

Essentially, the real draw of the cityscape to even a normally observant person is that the islands are not hidden from view; they are right downtown and virtually smack you in the face when you step out of your hotel. The fact that the coastline and islands are part of everyday life, embedded in the subconscious of the locals, and that the sensuous enjoyment of sandy beaches is so decidedly commonplace, is the true charm of the city. The islands, together with their determined band of inhabitants and grassy knolls, are a fitting symbol for the city: life-giving, durable, and timeless.

In fact, here in Zhuhai, the islands are not just scenic spots for sunshine and gorgeous beaches. They are the flesh and blood of the city, the incarnation of its vibrant now and hopeful future; they ARE the city.

The islands, together with their determined band of inhabitants and grassy knolls, are a fitting symbol for the city: life-giving, durable, and timeless.

BAYS & BEACHES

SONG OF THE SEA

Yeli Island

野狸島

In the eyes of the locals, the island is primarily a scenic park for a leisurely walk after dinner.

If complete isolation from the mainland, being reachable only by boat, is an essential requirement for inclusion in your "island itinerary" in Zhuhai, then perhaps Yeli isn't for you. If, on the other hand, you can open up your view a bit, you can appreciate the charm of the city's Yeli Island, ideally positioned only a few hundred meters away from the city's "beating heart", feeling as if it were placed by the Creator to be "the eye of the city," from which the inviting waterfront vista radiates to all corners.

The island's real name, "Yeli", as well as its "island" nature, seem to have long ago sunken into the subconscious of the locals, due to its close proximity to the city. So, if you feel the need to ask the way from the locals, referring to it as "Mingting Park" may be the more effective way of ensuring an accurate response. In fact, "Mingting Park" has almost become the synonym of "Yeli" and, in the eyes of the locals the island is primarily a scenic park for a leisurely walk after dinner.

The 0.3-square-kilometer, petite island used to be

easily accessible from the middle section of the seaside Love Promenade via Haiyan Bridge (literally "Sea Swallow Bridge"), a 340-meter-long span opened to traffic in 1995 as the only way to get to the island from the city proper. But the new Xinyue Bridge ("New Moon" Bridge) was unveiled in 2016, marking the retirement of Haiyan Bridge.

The island, or the "park", hosts the city's most eye-catching landmark, Zhuhai Opera House, known as the "shell"—the country's only city theater built on an island. Sitting majestically on a prime piece of real estate, the opera house sizzles with a dizzying variety of cultural events throughout the year, and is the indisputable symbol of the city's extraordinary taste.

The sprawling lawns along the 3.5-kilometer-long orbit road are perfect for kite flying, and seafront walkways and trails on the hillsides are favorite destinations for morning exercise. The user-friendly island is also favored by night joggers.

BAYS & BEACHES

淇澳岛
BRAVE HEART
Qi'ao Island

BRAVE HEART—QI'AO ISLAND

In that it takes only 60 seconds to drive from Tangjia Town to the cragged coast of Qi'ao Island, it barely passes for an "island". The 1,486-meter Qi'ao Bridge connecting it with downtown Zhuhai, together with all the maritime cultural attractions you'd expect to find on a sea island, has made Qi'ao the backyard garden of Zhuhai.

Strolling along the wild flower-strewn Qi'ao Island, a picturesque maritime hamlet located in the heart of the Guangdong-Hong Kong-Macao "triangle", one can't help but notice the lush foliage that gracefully hugs the craggy cliff-side. The breeze gathers pace around you, and the flowers and leaves begin to ripple, as if enacting a kind of floral Mexican wave.

The luxuriant old banyan trees, together with chirping nestlings, dragonflies and butterflies dancing with the tempo of the sea sprays, bespeak the unparalleled natural ecology of Qi'ao Island. The crystal spring streaming down the Wangchi Hill in the northeast serves as one of the water sources for the islanders, producing sweet water that perfectly matches first-class Pu'er tea.

A large number of ceramic findings at Housha Bay and the Dong'ao Bay show that the island is the earliest human habitat in today's Zhuhai. The unrivaled natural resources and environment remain so intact that the island hosts the country's largest mangrove forest park and a national Chinese White Dolphin Protection Base, launched in 2010.

The seafaring "golden oldies" of the island are more than well accommodated, spending their twilight years congregating for mahjong and trading stories of their turbulent oceanic adventures. Carrying out their daily tasks in an unrushed, methodical manner, the natives are unaware of what vast potential this one-time fishing village holds—something that the local government as well as a growing number of weary urbanites are keenly aware of.

For the time being, the island's oriental, maritime splendor is pretty much still intact, although tourist barges may outnumber fishing trawlers at some points in the year. Many of the coffee shops and B&B places here are open only on weekends.

The charming fishing village has an intriguing history of swashbuckling British opium traders, bewitching Temple of the Queen of Heaven and death-defying fishermen intent on bringing the mother-of-all hauls back to shore before sundown.

Every nook and cranny along the historical Baishi Street ensures aesthetic surprises.

BAISHI STREET

The bravery and wits of the islander's ancestors are etched in Baishi Street, a 2,000-meter footpath built by the inhabitants using 3,000 taels of silver taken from the British opium smugglers as compensation in the summer of 1836. Although there is no official written record about this heroic episode of the island, the very existence of the Jinxingjiao (once an opium smuggling post used by British and American merchants) and the island's costal defense remnants serve as convincing evidence that it is not a wildly inventive legend.

The snaking street with countless turnings is ideal for an aimless walk and constant, pleasant confusion. Every nook and cranny along the stretch ensures aesthetic surprises. The age-old wells hidden in thick woods are still used daily by the islanders.

The former residence of Su Zhaozheng (an early leader of the Communist Party of China and labor movement activist born on the island) awaits at the end of the street, as if to add a grand finishing touch to your "petty bourgeoisie" stroll. The six-lane shorefront orbit road perfumed with salty sea air wakes you up from the semi-hibernation induced by the bewitching street.

Lane Cottage B&B, 66 Baishi Street, Qi'ao Island. Tourists are advised to call for room reservation because most of the cafes and B&B places on the street are open only on weekends.

The snaking street with countless turnings is ideal for an aimless walk and constant, pleasant confusion.

Mangrove Wetland Park

BAYS & BEACHES

Calm and strange is this evening hour in the forest,
Carven domes of green are the trees by the pathway,
Infinite shadowy isles lie silent before me,
Summer is heavy with age, and leans upon Autumn,
All the land is ripe. There is no motion.
Down the long bays of blue that those cloudy headlands
Sleep above in the glow of a fading sunset;
All things rest in the will of purpose triumphant.
Outlines melting into a vague immensity,
Fade, the green gloom grows darker, and deeper the dusk:
Hark! A voice and laughter—the living and loving
Down these fantastic avenues pass like shadows.

— *Forest Picture* by Dylan Thomas

MANGROAVE WETLAND PARK

Nestled in the northwest of the island is China's largest mangrove forest, sure to color your voyage in this intoxicatingly beautiful saline corner of Zhuhai.

The 5,000-hectare, waterlogged sprawl that hosts 700 hectares of the salt-tolerant trees, adapted to life in harsh coastal conditions and containing a complex salt filtration and root system that copes with salt water immersion and wave action, is a testament to the superior ecology of Zhuhai and beautiful illustration of the city's "green" craze.

The swamp is also the first mangrove biome to have been artificially and successfully restored in China, and is an internationally recognized model of harmony between humans and nature.

Those who can't wait to peek into the forest will simply have to be patient; it is now in its rehabilitation phase and not open to visitors. Welsh poet and writer Dylan Thomas's *Forest Picture* mirrors the enchanting beauty of the natural reserve.

DEJA

BAYS & BEACHES

外伶仃島

Wailingding Island

Most of the people know Wailingding Island because of its historical connection with Wen Tianxiang (1236-1283) **, remembered as one of the "Three Loyal Princes of the Song Dynasty" (alongside Lu Xiufu and Zhang Shijie), and the Song patriot's famous quotation: "All men are mortal, but my loyalty will illuminate the annals of history forever".

In 1278, when Wen Tianxiang was captured by the invading Yuan armies of Kublai Khan, he refused to surrender and rejected an offer of a Yuan post, suffering four years in a military prison before his execution in 1283. One day in 1279 during his imprisonment on a Yuan boat that was passing the Lingding Channel, Wen wrote the woeful "Passing Lingdingyang".

With bountiful natural assets, Wailingding Island is indisputably the blue-eyed boy of Nature among the city's 147 islands (covering over 500sqm). With its northern wing only six sea miles from Hong Kong's Lantau and Tseung Kwan O, the island used to be an important military and trade fortress, something that seems hard to believe considering the island's current laid-back vibe.

It takes a little climbing along the trails at Lingding Peak, better known as "Shijing Park" among tourists and islanders, for a taste of the island's stormy past in a subtle and organic way.

In a sense, the island is

A bustling scene at the Wailingding Square, where the dock and an array of tourism facilities are sited, and much of the islanders' daily chores unfold

---

** <u>Wen Tianxiang</u>'s life and poetry are well-documented in Western academic circles, with WEN T'IEN-HSIANG: A Biographical Study of a Song Patriot by Brown, William Andreas (1986) being a brilliant example.

an elegy to the undying patriotism of Wen Tianxiang, and rightly so. More than 700 years after his beheading, the little nameless flowers and weeds serve as the most fitting symbol for this beguiling place. One cannot help but be enchanted by the robust plants that remain tightly huddled together despite the powerful, easterly gusts. "They are survivors," said a local onlooker cryptically, sauntering off into the distance.

In the old times, long before Hong Kong's return, the incessant traffic stream of Kowloon and the hubbub on the Tsing Ma Bridge—the most prominent element of the Lantau Link in Hong Kong—looming phantasmagorically in the undulating mists beyond the horizon, was charmingly mistaken by the unsophisticated residents of Wailingding as a mirage. The contours of skyscrapers, hills and bridges beyond the cobalt blue waters created a surreal, daily visual feast that once immensely fascinated the fishing villagers, who may never have realized that their own homeland was also a "mirage" in the eyes of the people living across the ocean.

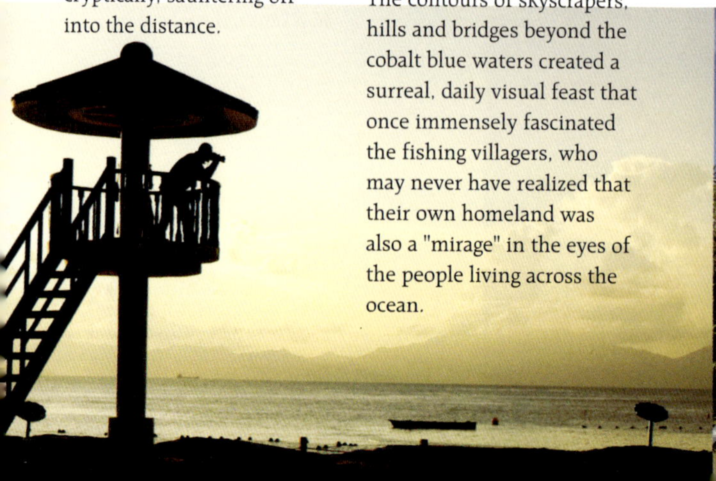

The "mirage" beyond the horizon easily makes one fall into a reverie.

Soak in the dreamy sea vista at the oceanfront terrace of Xiangsiling Seaview Villa Hotel.

Set against the evening twilight, the grotesque rocks that form the craggy coasts feel like the Mediterranean setting of Alexendre Duma's, *The Count of Monte Cristo*.

BAYS & BEACHES

The "mirage" beyond the horizon easily makes one fall into a reverie.

Soak in the dreamy sea vista at the oceanfront terrace of Xiangsiling Seaview Villa Hotel.

The fishing bustle behind the island's seafood market that sits north of the dock is hard to miss.

The 4.23-square-kilometer island is largely hilly and rocky, which makes the flat ground where the dock is sited a natural gathering spot for leisure and business. The island's breezy alleys and the only "bookstore on an island" in Zhuhai, together with the fishing bustle behind the island's seafood market that sits north of the dock, are hard or even impossible to miss. Before it joined the city's vibrant marine tourism scene, Wailingding was purely a fishing island. Its seafaring glory is still obvious in the island's fishing business quarter near the dock. For more gastronomically motivated visitors, it is fortunately never short of the "three treasures of Wailingding" ("general's hat", sea urchin and "dog paw snail"), and ensures a wonderful ocean-to-table dining experience.

Set against the evening twilight, the grotesque rocks that form the craggy coasts feel like the Mediterranean setting of Alexandre Duma's, *The Count of Monte Cristo*. And the view at the Gothic-style, winding staircase of a neat, dependable hotel set against a backdrop of infinite green and blue is timeless.

READZONE's Wailingding location, the only "bookstore on an island" in Zhuhai.

Set against the evening twilight, the grotesque rocks that form the craggy coasts feel like the Mediterranean setting of Alexandre Duma's, *The Count of Monte Cristo*.

BAYS & BEACHES

DEJA VU——WAILINGDING ISLAND

CASTLE ON

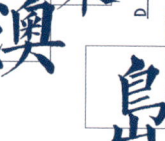
東澳島 Dong'ao Island

BAYS & BEACHES

Some 30 sea miles southeast from the Port of Xiangzhou lies a mythical oasis that is a heady mix of sunshine, sand and soul-reaching sea air. As boat pulls in to shore, you will plunge into air so sweet that your lungs ache with joy. No need to worry about sunburn—the island has a forest coverage rate of more than 80%.

The intoxicating beauty of the 4-square-kilometer "Shangri La" can be relished from many different angles, whether it is a bird's-eye view of the seascape from Fudan Peak or watching the crimson sun rising from the horizon at the lovely Dong'ao Bay, a 1,500-meter concavity on the eastern side of the island. The bay area has since ancient times been a port of call because of its calm waters and tranquility. Today, the bay is the island's "comfort zone" that hosts the island market, tourist dock and a string of restaurants and grocery stores.

On a ridge high above the sheltering cove, the Chongcheng Castle (built in 1729) records a stirring chapter in the islanders' home defense. The castle's remains became one of

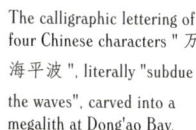
The calligraphic lettering of four Chinese characters "万海平波", literally "subdue the waves", carved into a megalith at Dong'ao Bay.

BAYS & BEACHES

the first historical sites to be given city-level cultural protection as early as 1987. Elsewhere, a number of ex-military shelters and entrenchments, together with the debris of a customs establishment built in 1898, give visitors a taste of the island's warring past and former glory as an important trading post.

In its heyday in the Ming and Qing times, the island was home to some 3,000 inhabitants and abuzz with the comings-and-goings of ships, fishermen and military men. With the islanders uprooting themselves in warring chaos, the island fell deserted and was eventually taken over by a totally different food chain - dominated by plants.

In 1796, the first year of Emperor Jiaqing (1760-1820) of the Qing Dynasty, pirate Zhang Baozai, on a whim, ordered his military counsellor to do something to sing praises of his unquestionably thriving piratical career. The result was the calligraphic lettering of four Chinese characters "万海平波", literally "subdue the waves", carved into a megalith at Dong'ao Bay. Two decades later, this pirate

leader claiming to be "a true man" saw his spirited maritime business completely wiped out. Legend has it that, knowing the game was as good as lost, Zhang buried 18 boxes of treasure on the island and that the location and password is encrypted in one of the four characters on the megalith, insinuated by the plum-flower patterns.

The swashbuckler, film-style fantasy, as well as the walk-on-air mood of this Chinese "Captain Jack Sparrow", can be savored by today's people at the precipitous southern tip of the island's orbit seaside road. In the clashing waves clapping hard onto the reefs, one can still sense the overwhelming ambition of Zhang Baozai in his most glamorous years.

Climate and elevation is perfect here, making the island a popular tourist destination during the period from June to October. To capture the island's distinctive allure and windswept grace, one is advised to head down to the "diamond beach", where the soft, soft sands that cannot be found anywhere else in the Wanshan Archipelago almost melt in the temperature of your palms and refresh the body, mind and soul in an instant. The picture-perfect sea view ensures a trance-like

state of absent-mindedness.

Don't leave the island without a stroll along the 11.8-km hillside orbit trail that stretches from Nansha Bay to the tourist dock. The rocky northern tip of the trail is reminiscent of the Cape of Good Hope.

In the same manner that restaurants have their own signature dishes that you simply must try, a quaintly-named shellfish that tastes like the best abalone you can find in this world is the island's other undisputed star. The best season to try this delicacy, fondly called "general's hat", is in winter.

Tourists are served by a host of neat hotels, including the stylish Gree Dong'ao Hotel, all sited in the "diamond beach" area. The picture-perfect view outside the floor-to-ceiling window of the hotel is a marvelous spectacle, one you may have seen only in your dreams.

The waves here have a pleasant tension that is ideal for the more adventurous beach swimmers and water sports enthusiasts. For the more faint-hearted, Monte Carlo Bar's signature Mojito delights all the senses.

THE SUN ALSO

Dawanshan Island

大萬山島

To reach authentic beauty, there is always a price to pay, and this is proven again by the one-hour of light-headedness on a boat that takes you from the Xiangzhou Port in the city proper to Dawanshan (literally "Big Wanshan") Island. Your seasickness, however, will be washed away right upon arrival at this fantastic site as colorful as an oil painting. The island is home to China's best-conserved spectacle from the quaternary glacier, and is THE place to marvel at the magic of marine corrosion.

** Dreamland Hotels & Resorts, reputed as "a resort born from trees and rocks", is managing three boutique hotels on Dawanshan Island, Doumen and Wailingding Island, and three stylish restaurants (Verona, Chiba, Harbor View) in Zhuhai.

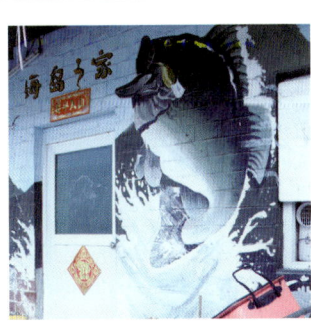

Despite the fact that the island has no sand beach for bikini shows, its primitive beauty has drawn attention from both the city's tourism committee and vigilant investors. Tourists here are served by The Dreamland Resort**, a chic boutique hotel that is truly "built into" the island. The construction took only one year to complete, with the original vegetation on the island perfectly preserved. The result is a hotel that truly "grows with nature" and feels like a botanical wonderland, with a gorgeous infinity pool lying under the shade of an ancient banyan tree.

Originally called Laowanshan (literally "Old Wanshan"), Dawanshan became a human settlement around 1785, in the years of Emperor Qianlong in the Qing Dynasty. Its far-flung location endows the island with a pristine quality that culminates at the Fushi (literally "floating stones") Bay on the treacherous southeastern side of the island. Dubbed "a wonder in Asia", the site is a "restricted zone" that shows the uncanny workmanship of Nature in full play and

would make you weak at the knees. The creepy sound created by tidal waves flooding into the crevices adds a veil of mystery to the place. Standing here, one seems to be standing at the ends of the earth. For the more adventurous, it is a pity that the site is not open to tourists, but even a bird's eye view from the watch-house nearing the highest peak of the island is enough to take your breath away.

Another interesting spot to check out is Xiaowanshan ("Lesser Wanshan"), a dreamy haven that sits a crescent body of water away and takes only a few minutes

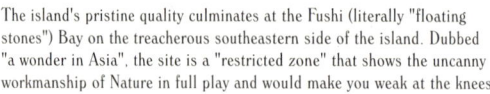

The island's pristine quality culminates at the Fushi (literally "floating stones") Bay on the treacherous southeastern side of the island. Dubbed "a wonder in Asia", the site is a "restricted zone" that shows the uncanny workmanship of Nature in full play and would make you weak at the knees.

on a speed ferry to reach from Dawanshan. Setting foot in Xiaowanshan feels like walking haphazardly into the previous life of the "Wanshan" islanders. In an unspoiled wilderness, lush with all sorts of unfamiliar plants, everything seems to be a freeze-frame from a hundred years ago. Only the flocks of goats unwatched by their Dawanshan owners bring you back to reality.

The Mazu Temple that sits in a prominent seaside position has been providing the islanders with spiritual protection from the fearsome waters beyond for only-God-knows how many years. Here, local maidens would pray for the safe return of their brave and hardworking fathers, brothers and lovers; and fishermen from Macao, Hong Kong and elsewhere on the southern China coast would congregate on the 23rd day of the third lunar month (according to the Chinese lunar calendar), the most important day in a year for the locals. Hilarious lion dances and colorful, earthy sea-themed decorations on the door create an abundance of atmosphere, and are harbingers of Wanshan's hard-fishin' glory.

Located at the Pearl River Delta's southern tip, where the waters of the Pearl River meet the waves of the South China Sea, this gem of the "City of a Hundred Islands" is justifiably the jewel in Zhuhai's salty crown. With as many as five bays in its territory, the Wanshan area has long hosted a smorgasbord of marine life. In the 1980s, the local fishermen broke a national single catch record.

Unique location and rich marine resources also make Dawanshan one of the country's top three offshore fishing grounds, drawing in daredevil anglers from all over the world. Offshore fishing fanatics flood here on January 1 every year for an "angling carnival" to indulge in the thrill of challenging

Infinity Pool at The Dreamland Resort, Dawanshan.

(Right) A bird's eye view of the island from the watch-house nearing its highest peak.

tempestuous waves just for the excitement of it.

The region is also a paradise for what may be the country's best seafood, and was featured in the second season of the sensational CCTV documentary, *A Bite of China*. The groupers and wild sea urchin here, if you come in the right season, melt in your mouth like a Hershey bar. "Notoriously" nicknamed by Westerners as "seafood from hell", the "dog claw snail", thriving in the riff crevices, is convincing physical evidence of the pollution-free marine ecology of Wanshan. If you come here in the 3.5-month fishing "off season", (from May 1 to mid-August) of the South China Sea, conch whistle hawkers, a number of ocean themed trinket sellers and the seaweed soup crafted by the chef at the Dreamland Resort await to make up for the scarcity of many other seasonal delicacies.

Each of the outdoor terraces, tailor-made for the 30 stylish guestrooms at The Dreamland Resort, ensures an unforgettable sunrise memory. Afterwards, throw yourself into the inviting waters of the resort's infinity swimming pool, and feel the embrace of heaven.

THE SUN ALSO RISES—DAWANSHAN ISLAND

BAYS & BEACHES

THE SUN ALSO RISES—DAWANSHAN ISLAND

廟灣島

BAYS & BEACHES

BLEU, BLANC, ROUGE

Miaowan Island

Your encounter with this lovely islet, sitting far out in open waters, feels like the chance discovery of the Peach Blossom Land described by the Jin poet, Tao Yuanming (365-427). The farthest one in the Wanshan Archipelago, Miaowan has been known for its illusive beauty and mystery. The area's crystal-clear water, free of pollution, makes the hard-to-reach island a true paradise for seasoned sea anglers and deep diving fanatics.

Anonymity is what this "lost world" has going for it, stealing your heart and making you want to return soon, for the soothing caress of the salty air, the pristine water at the Xiafengwan bathing beach, the chatty owner of the QQ Seafood Restaurant, and the gentle rustle of the sea sprays lilting in the welcome summer breeze.

Miaowan is the only accessible island in the Zhuhai territory that takes a speed boat, or "dafei" (a slang favored by the locals), to reach from the city proper. The frantically bumpy 90-minute journey from the Yinkeng Dock is a joyful experience for the more adventurous, but a hard-learned lesson for the squeamish. The boat jolts along the rough, endless sea, braving the wind with the engine making deafening sounds throughout the journey.

"How far is it to the island?" I asked in a daze.

"It's right in front of you," The guy at the helm shot back lightly.

"Where?" I persisted.

"As far as the eye can see," he explained with a smile.

At the finishing line of the mad dash that not only washes away all your make-up but drains all your energy, you will be awakened by a small, boisterous crowd at the QQ Seafood Restaurant run by a curly-haired, chatty guy and his neat, light-footed wife, whose magic hands make the world's best "sea urchin with steamed egg" and pan-fried sole fish. The dining space overlooks a mesmerizing sand beach that takes a little walking along the hillside to reach.

Lying in the wide-open spaces of the deep sea, this primitive haven of peace and tranquility is a joy to behold, and the fantastic view of the Xiafeng Bay corallaceous sandbeach is a convincing illustration of the allusion to Maldives.

Make your way up to a corner of the reef toward the dock and the island's residential dwellings, and a modest but significant lighthouse appears, first built by the Brits in 1884, nodding to the island's hard-working, hard-fishing former glory.

Miaowan Island is not for those looking for urban amenities and hotel luxuries, but an ideal retreat for those in need of a dose of solitude. Forget Wifi-fuelled connectivity from the comfort of your rickety outdoor stools. Electricity and tap water is in limited supply. The only sound that penetrates the beautiful silence is your heartbeat; and the best thing to do here is nothing at all.

Try making "Uncle Handsome", the island's telecommunication tower watchman tipsy, and he will squint his eyes and share all the untold stories of the island and its proud fisherman heritage. Considering the island's colorful maritime history of strong-jawed fishermen and violent offshore storms that could kill a boatful of men in the blink of an eye, whatever weird story the man chooses to share with a bewildered tourist would be within the realm of possibility.

The island's natives, mostly elderly, can be counted on one's fingers, friendly and always happily surprised to see visitors, as if unaware of the outside world for decades. Doors are left unbolted at night. Honesty prevails throughout. For the indigenous people here, the island's position in the blueprint of the city's marine tourism is less important than living for today.

The island is left untouched by the groping hands of holiday makers and tourism investors.

The island is peaceful and pleasingly gritty, left untouched by the groping hands of holiday makers and tourism investors. The old folks—pensioners with weathered faces and thousand-yard stares—seem to be immune to today's lightening-fast development and sizzling investments transpiring across the strait, intent instead on seeing out their days in the exact same way they've spent the last six decades or so—at their own leisure. The absence of luxury hotels and convenience stores makes for an authentic Chinese seaside experience, and the growing bustle from casual visitors is a sure sign that new life is slowly being breathed into the islet.

The rocky, two-square-kilometer island is humble, earthy and easy to miss like a roadside wild flower, but what it lacks in razzle-dazzle more than makes up for an unassuming beauty, and possesses a kind of reluctant allure that more sensitive souls can easily appreciate.

The dining space of the QQ Seafood Restaurant overlooks a mesmerizing sand beach that takes a little walking along the hillside to reach.

The fantastic view of the Xiafeng Bay corallaceous sandbeach is a convincing illustration of the allusion to Maldives.

CRYSTAL-CLEAR

BAYS & BEACHES

A LIFE-GIVING CITY
ZHUHAI'S EVER-EXPANDING PARKLAND GRID
A RIVER RUNS THROUGH IT

A LIFE-GIV

A LIVABLE CITY

Le gend has it that the vast blue and mystical scent of orchid blossoms in the abyss of Fenghuang Mountain once enchanted the youngest daughter of the Dragon King of the South China Sea so much that the girl never returned to where she belonged. "Sea" is the soul and its hue the true color of the city.

When Italian writer Italo Calvino finished his fantasy quest for urban perfection in *Invisible Cities* in 1972, with an imagined Marco Polo describing 55 fictitious cities, all with virtues but none complete, he had no way of knowing that over the next several decades a city would be developing that possessed a perfect blend of all the best features of those 55—Zhuhai. Even Kublai Khan, who was entertained in the novel by Marco's outlandish descriptions, would have to admit that Zhuhai is not just a "livable" city; it is life-giving, just like the sea.

ING CITY

Home to a comparatively large Cantonese-speaking demographic, Zhuhai is something of a cultural melting pot as immigrants form the majority of its approximately 1.7 million current inhabitants. The city's unique cultural diversity permeates all aspects of its social and economic life, as illustrated in its rich cuisine and lively cultural scene, inextricably connected with its prominent historical positioning as one of the country's former seafaring centers and a pioneer of China's modernization in both industrial and educational senses.

The city might not capture your heart immediately; rather, it seduces its visitors slowly, via osmosis, as the newcomer soaks in the unique blend of pleasing features, day after day. Over time, its captivating landscapes, balmy weather, well-protected marine cultural legacy (embodied in countless points-of-interest), culinary splendor and, of course, the charming flora including mangrove wonderlands, all add up to get under your skin. And, of course, there is the charming "lazy sound" characteristic of its Cantonese-dominated language—the de facto official spoken form of the Chinese language used in the Hong Kong government and as the medium of instruction in schools, alongside English.

In Zhuhai, pinpointing the moment that the "concrete jungle" disappears and the seascape

begins, is nearly a futile task because at least half of the city lies up close to the caressing waves of the ocean. Here, everything around you seems to slow down, ease off and settle into an altogether more laid-back groove. A walk on its unrivaled seaside boulevard is proof enough of the city's easy-going romance with life. The noise and bustle that normally accompanies the day-to-day routine in contemporary China seems to fade away.

The lifestyle here, however, defies the simple label of "slow-paced". Essentially, the city is defined by its unspoiled authenticity—its noticeable and consistent effort to shun overheated renovation and fancy-pants gentrification. Economic revitalization does not occur at the sudden and isolated behest of local cultural and architectural landmarks but, rather, develops in tandem with the love for cultural heritage and desire to preserve the best of it. Beneath the city's soothing base color is a truly organic kernel that keeps tradition settled and deep-rooted, producing a city that is organically balanced in a way that visitors will find utterly captivating. The time-freezing, life-giving grace behind the city's blue and green façade holds your imagination hostage for the duration of your stay.

The well-retained scenic and cultural authenticity of Zhuhai offers food for thought for those interested in the balance between rampant development and heartfelt conventionality—a hot topic in these turbulent times.

In 1998, Zhuhai was recognized by the United Nations Centre for Human Settlements (UNCHS) for its exemplary accomplishments in improving the living conditions in urban centers.

New shoots and fresh buds after Super Typhoon Hato stretched itself over the city in the mid-summer of 2017. The response of volunteerism that met the damage and destruction of the storm revealed a shared sense of pride in and care for the place all people in Zhuhai call home.

A LIFE-GIVING CITY

The coasts and the city's mountainous surroundings are a botanical treasure house. Rare subtropical flora and fauna can be admired amidst steaming greenery and various unspoiled oases. The villages and their environs are strewn with thousand-year-old trees that act as living witnesses to the city's unfailing splendor.

The primitive wetlands found in the mountain valleys near the city really kick off your jungle adventure in style. Places abound where the passes become quite rugged and hiking turns into the real "Man vs Wild" stuff. Handling the treacherous cliffs and age-old plank roads is no easy task for inexperienced outdoor enthusiasts.

Bauhinia variegata (Purple Orchid Tree), a very popular ornamental tree in subtropical and tropical climates, grown for its scented flowers

ZHUHAI'S EVER-EXPANDING PARKLAND GRID

Central Park in Manhattan, New York City, located between the Upper West Side and Upper East Side, is the most visited urban park in the United States and one of the most filmed locations in the world. The park's size and cultural position, similar to London's Hyde Park and Munich's Englischer Garten, have served as a model for many urban parks. Widely recognized as the world's first urban park in the truest sense of the word, it serves as a beautiful illustration of that potential symbiotic bond between parks and a city; and in this sense, Zhuhai stands out among China's most livable cities with its "greensward plan" which has virtually turned the whole city into an extended, inter-connected parkland.

Visiting a selection from the city's wide choice of parklands ought to be a priority for those traveling or living in Zhuhai. For first-time visitors, the pleasant size of the city is ideal to explore by simply snooping around, not aimlessly but with a sense of willful abandon. Choose a point on the map, try to get there somehow, and you will find that there is always an empty bench awaiting under an exuberant banyan tree for you to take a breather and stretch your legs after going through the exasperation of modern-day air travel.

With plenty of places to sit and admire the captivating city views, its unusually large number of parks becomes obvious as a clear selling point for Zhuhai. Each of these urban oases is a place where you can easily lose track of time (so do be careful if you have to keep on schedule). All popular but not overcrowded, well-maintained but not sterile, the parks in Zhuhai are resplendent with life.

The hope to make Zhuhai a "park city" is the force behind a community park movement that started in 2012, and has so far spawned more than 100 parks across the city. The goal is to turn all the city's fringes and refuse sites into greenbelts and continuously increase the total number of parks.

The city's Love Promenade, stringing a cluster of urban parks together, is in effect China's longest parkland. Low-lying Banzhang Mountain, stretching along the picturesque seaside boulevard, is a forest park in its own right and has given birth to a cycle of urban parks in the core urban area of Xiangzhou.

Occupying a corner of Banzhang Mountain, Shijingshan Park was established in 1987 and has since been serving as a downtown leisure spot. One can either take the cable or walk to the park's apex to take in the classic skyline and graceful coasts of Xianglu Bay. Continue the walk southwards along Jingshan Road, Bailian Road and Jiuzhou Avenue, and you'll be bathed in the archaic air of lovely temples and a lily-perfumed pond, legendarily created by resident monks in the Qianlong years of the Qing Dynasty.

Shijingshan Park is bordered on the west by the iconic New Yuanming Palace, the Zhuhai version of the original Summer Palace in Beijing. Nestled in the gorgeous natural setting of this "lake park" is the Zhuhai campus of Jinan University.

The northern side of Banzhang Mountain hosts Shixi Park, where a man of letters in the Qing Dynasty was convinced that the scenery was a virtual twin for the landscape around Kuaiji Hill, in the outskirts of present-day Shaoxing, which had inspired China's greatest

calligrapher to accomplish his masterpiece on a fine, late spring day in the year 353. The ebullient mood of the Qing literati who were so impressed by the coursing streams, lush woods and peculiar rocks that they couldn't restrain themselves in verse can be savored by people today at various points of interest, accompanied by calligraphic traces of their literary joy.

A hillside trail leads to Dajingshan, the city's largest "sports park", built around the Dajingshan Reservoir. The 80,000-sq. m grassy sprawl hosts four football fields, five basketball courts, a volleyball court and an indoor playground—all quite ideal for informal or team sports, with many quiet areas set aside for joggers, cyclists and skateboarders.

The Meihua Urban Park, stretching some 200,000sqm, contains a full range of sports facilities, beautifully positioned alongside a large area of banana and papaya woods. What was once a vast expanse of desolate wildness has been transformed into an "urban garden" with a very natural feel.

Tucked away at the northeastern tip of Banzhang Mountain is Xiangshan Park. You can grab a coffee at the READZONE Bookstore near the entrance of the park before the climb into the dense woods, known for its engaging beauty and tranquility. The parks, blending into the southern wing of Banzhang Mountain, constitute another of the city's "green screens", woven seamlessly into the daily goings-on of the old-town quarters of Zhuhai. The hilltops of Shihuashan Park, Jiangjunshan Park and Paotaishan Park all serve as natural viewing decks for the fabulous urban contours of Macao just across the shimmering body of waters.

For a taste of the authentic grass-roots city life of Zhuhai, the Paotaishan Park (literally "Cannon Platform Park") is a fitting place to check out. Surveying the woods, quiet nooks and enclosed playgrounds, burbling with the laughter of frolicking children, you'll meet people walking backwards, grannies dancing to hot-blooded pop, rosy-cheeked tai-chi

gurus, and fluffy puppies with fancy clothes.

Outside the Xiangzhou area, the sheer size of the city's parklands is eye-opening for people from the country's concrete jungles. Located in Doumen, Jianfengshan Forest Park is the largest of its kind in Guangdong Province. The 171-hectare lot is still expanding.

The city's rich wetland resources have also blossomed into a cluster of parks that are all paradises for water-loving plants and avian life, with natural-looking lakes and ponds that have been created artificially by damming natural seeps and flows. A world-class wetland landscaping project, the Seaside Wetland Park in Hengqin hosts two zones, named Mangzhou (literally "Mango Oasis") and Erjingwan.

The city's ambitious "park map" will also see two new significant members joining in soon: the wetland park set in Jinwan Aviation Town and Hengqin Central Park in Hengqin New Area, both promising to create a grid of expansive, luxuriant greenness for all settlers in the city's new urban centers and showing the world how an "Adelaide Parklands"** can arise on the southern coasts of China.

** Adelaide, the capital city of the state of South Australia and widely recognized as one of the world's most livable cities, is a planned city, designed by the first Surveyor-General of South Australia, Colonel William Light. His plan, now known as Light's Vision, arranged Adelaide in a grid, with five squares in the Adelaide city centre and a ring of parks, known as the Adelaide Parklands, surrounding it.

Qianshan A RIVER RUN

He who has sailed the seven seas doesn't think much of mere rivers.

Qianshan River

Rising from the dense forests on the southeast side of Wugui Mountain in neighboring Zhongshan City, the Qianshan River feeds into the great mouth of the Pearl River Delta and is the only freshwater river within Zhuhai territory. The 41-km waterway runs through three cities: Zhongshan, Zhuhai and Macao, with some 8 kilometers of that in Zhuhai.

A major water clean-up campaign was launched by the city government in 2005 to restore the water quality of the city's "mother river" (actually, that of both Zhuhai and Macao). The success of that project, together with the city's pro-active implementation of many other water governance schemes, brought Zhuhai into the select group of "National Pilot Cities for Water Eco-civilization Construction" in 2015.

A RIVER RUNS THROUGH IT

前山河

*Lo*ng, long ago, the Qianshan River was called the "Qianshan Sea". In a vigorous wave of reclamation during the late Ming and early Qing times, this vast expanse of waters was reshaped into an inland waterway.

In both functional and psychological senses, the river has always been the lifeline of Zhuhai and an important, if rather under-appreciated, part of the local consciousness and identity, gently nourishing this remarkable coastal settlement and presenting a fantastic "tale of two cities" with Zhuhai and Macao sitting on opposite sides of this shared river.

Let your heart be guided by the waters, and you will come to understand the symbiotic bond between a river and its people, and appreciate the resilient and enduring heart of a river that is often, dismissively, referred to as just a "waterway", stressing its great utility but losing much of the romance and tradition.

The fact that the river was reduced to a polluted nuisance in the 1990s does not for a moment diminish its persevering vitality. The river's rebirth in the new millennium, thanks to the city's commitment to water ecology regulation, only adds to its stature and renewed sheen. Through the clarity of the glassy water, one can see the gathering potential of the city's future.

The meandering course of the river provides an ideal route for tourists who hope to get a convenient fish-eye view of the southwest side of the city's bustling Xiangzhou District. An afternoon stroll along the delightful banks— in any kind of weather (but ideally stormy, speaking from our recent experiences)— provides all sorts of insights and revelations regarding the relationship between people and "their" river.

A 1,387-meter span opened to traffic in 2017, the quaint Baishi Bridge, immersed in dark clouds gathering and billowing overhead, feels at first sight like a mirage resembling the London Bridge.

We are all deeply connected to the land where we grew up but, if a river runs through it, like a seam of emotional gold, it attaches to you in a way that is deeper yet. A river that runs through a city, remaining essentially the same despite all the changes that surround it over the years, has always got a whiff of magic about it. In the 1992 movie, *A River Runs Through It*, a young Brad Pitt is enchanted by the river running through his home town, and his family's story is woven around it. Near the end of the movie, his brother returns as an old man and, discovering that most of the people from his youth are gone, he is simultaneously haunted and comforted by those waters. Indeed, to have a river to come back to and be haunted by for life is a blessing, as all Zhuhai people may tell you.

Streaming eastward from the southeast side of Wugui Mountain in Zhongshan City into the territory of Zhuhai, the Qianshan River steers southward abruptly when reaching the Zhuhai Bridge, as if giving way to some kind of spell. The undercurrents turn wilder as the river bumps into Macao, where the waters roll westward before determinedly hurrying off into the South China Sea.

Fengshui experts reason that Fenghuang Mountain is the "provider" of Zhuhai (using fengshui terminology), and that the Qianshan River therefore brings fortune to the city. But the flow of fortune is "intercepted" by Macao at the estuary where the river joins the sea. Well, in the final analysis, Macao may be judged innocent; the way the two cities are connected is a natural and mutually beneficial creation that eventually puts all covetous thoughts to shame.

"Fortune", however, does not seem sufficient to describe what the river has brought to the city. The calm waters may seem benign now, but rewind several decades and the scene greeting you would be entirely different. The bulk of massive urban redevelopment and sweeping westward expansion in the wake of Special Economic Zone status being granted in 1980 hinged on this stretch of the river, with developments that profoundly changed the social fabric on both banks. Long serving as a vital source for irrigation and drinking water, the site sizzled with a new sort of activity when a pumping station was launched there in 1980 to direct water into Macao for the city's water supply.

Once upon a time, Qianshan River was also the city's urban and countryside watershed. Frolicking and catching fish in the rapids is a fond part of the childhood memory of the older generation there. When the

Nanping Bridge opened for traffic in 1987, villagers living in Beishan, up the northern reaches of the river, returned home carrying gongs and "lions" after a hilarious day celebrating the opening of the 532-meter span. With the distance between their rural homeland and the "city life" across the river being shortened overnight, it was time to say goodbye to ramshackle ferries for commuting. The bridge completed its mission on April 15, 2018, and is being replaced by an eight-lane passage, but the gurgling sound of water is still a reminder of the toil and industry that helped make this part of Zhuhai the beating heart of city life that it is today.

In the late 1980s and throughout the 1990s, the rapids of the river became further tamed and shrunken amidst the headlong rush of urbanization, bringing more transportation conveniences and amenities to the life of the residents on the west bank of the river and indeed the wider community. With a bridge network taking shape, west bank villagers no longer had to ride their old bikes to the Qianshan Dock and await a bumpy ferry ride to the "city" on the other side of the river for the weekend "brunch feast".

Arrive on the banks some stormy day, and the view from the Qianshan Bridge, not far from the Guangzhou-Zhuhai Intercity Railway Station, is the river's strangely unaccountable bend that seems oddly in-between, as it eventually blends into the old town sprawl in the north. The quaint Baishi Bridge, immersed in dark clouds gathering and billowing overhead, feels at first sight like a mirage resembling the London Bridge. The gusts gain momentum with each passing second. You might feel noticeable changes in mood and the heart may be filled with a nostalgic kind of joy. Pull over to the side to inspect a particularly twinkling stretch of glassy water; you almost feel whisked away to another province, time or country.

Walk further southward from the Baishi Bridge, and the vista opens up as the river

A LIVABLE CITY

A RIVER RUNS THROUGH IT

widens into the skylines of Macao in the distance. Even further southward along the bank, the water becomes a little more fierce, as if to brace up for a new territory: Macao. The southern tip of the waterway is a prime viewing spot to take in the spectacular neon jungle of the "sleepless Las Vegas of the Orient", once so close but so untouchable—now an easy walk away.

Today, the west riverfront that was once a vast unspoiled wilderness has been attractively remodeled with neat, wide decking for walkers and a forest of luxury river-view condo complexes connected with chic malls and a handful of exuberant parklands.

On the east side, the time-honored Qianshan River Construction Materials Market and the Xiawan Night Market—a hot venue among the city's night-owls—await to send you on a sentimental journey through the area's inviting history if you can tear yourself away from the river front. As you make your way off the riverside path towards the depths of the riverfront residences, the surrounding flora close in around you in a scene that would be reminiscent of a Grimm brothers fairytale.

The river is not a "river" in the strict sense of the word after it passes the Changsheng Bridge (literally "prosperity bridge"), opened in 2003, in the southernmost portion of the route. The view from the bridge is dominated by the glistening façade of the Grand Lisboa casino, feeling close enough to touch. People living in one of the high-rises in this neighborhood can relish the spectacle of the annual Macao International Fireworks Festival by just looking out of the window.

VI

Night at the Museum
A Peak into the Treasure Chest of Zhuhai

A Stroll into the Past
Shanfang Road Promenade

A Paradise for All
East and West, Home Is the Best.

A Family Above and Beyond
Beishan Village

Rising Wind and Flying Clouds
Huitong Village

Always Together, Forever Apart
Qixia Xianguan

Legend of Doumen
Doumen Old Street / Luyi Tang / Jintai Temple / Jiexia Estate

TALES
SECRETS

NIGHT AT THE

A Peak into the Trea

A stunning set of objects on display at the city's exquisite new museum takes the visitor on a hypnotizing trip back through time. The modern facade peels away quickly as you confront the evidence of those who lived in this same area as far back as 6,000 years ago, and the modern metropolis suddenly takes on a surprisingly antique character.

MUSEUM

...ure Chest of Zhuhai

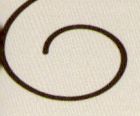

Painted Pottery

Four painted pottery items and a dozen fragments made approximately 6,000 years ago and excavated from the Housha Bay archeological site, these are the earliest and most representative discovered to date.

"TAO DOU"

Unearthed from the Baojing Bay site in Zhuhai. "Dou" was the name of food containers or sacrificial vessels in the ancient times of China. The craft of "dou" pottery dates back to the late Neolithic Age.

WHITE POTTERY "GUI"

A rare, successful restoration of one of the two White Pottery "gui" pieces excavated at the Housha Bay historic site in Zhuhai. "White pottery" features a white body and surface. This pitcher was used for boiling and storing liquids, and its shape indicates a surprisingly advanced level of pottery-making in this region during the late Neolithic Period.

Barkcloth Bat

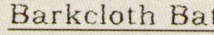

A barkcloth bat made of stone, found in the Zhuhai territory, is one of the earliest representatives of barkcloth craftsmanship. Barkcloth is a versatile material that was once common in Asia, Africa, Indonesia, and the Pacific. Barkcloth comes primarily from trees of the Moraceae family and is made by beating sodden strips of the fibrous inner bark of these trees into sheets, which are then finished into a variety of items.

Pottery Findings at Baojing Bay Site

Archeologists found a surprisingly huge pottery reserve at Baojing Bay, located in southwestern Gaolan Island in Zhuhai. In that most of the pottery pieces unearthed here are made of sandy clay, they are estimated to have been produced approximately 6,000 years ago.

STONE "BEN"

One of the most important tools invented in the Neolithic Age, "ben" was used for felling trees and wood processing by the Stone Age people.

Stone Spinning Wheel

An early device for spinning thread or yarn from natural fibers. More advanced spinning wheels were first used in India, between 500 and 1000 C.E and were replaced by spinning machinery during the Industrial Revolution. The stone spinning wheel indicates the very early spinning techniques used by people living in today's Zhuhai as early as 6,000-7,000 years ago.

Stone Fishing-net Weights

A large number of archeological sites representing a crucial period in the history of the Pearl River Delta (some 4,000 years ago) have been found within the Pearl River Delta territory. The sites yielded a sizable number of stone fishing-net weights, reflecting the bustling fishing industry of Zhuhai 4,000 years ago.

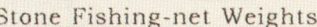

"YU JUE" (PENANNULAR JADE RING)

Known as the oldest type of jade ornament found in China, in ancient times, "jue" were used as earrings and bracelets.

Big-mouth "zun"

Many "ge", "zun", "dou" and other early pottery forms have been found, representing the Fubin stage of the middle and late Shang Dynasty culture on the east coast of Guangdong Province, and indicating early cultural exchange between eastern Guangdong and the Pearl River environs.

FOUR-EAR POT

Found by local fishermen in the sea near Hebao Island in Zhuhai, this piece testifies to the long-standing trade and communication between China and Southeast Asia, as well as Western countries, via this "pottery road on the sea".

"Shi fan"

A mould-style tool used to make bronze-ware in early times. Bronze excavations from the Guangdong area have yielded only a small number of these, representing the Wucheng Civilization in the late Shang Dynasty (1600-1046 BC).

ROCK ETCHINGS

The seven sets of rock etchings discovered at the Baojing Bay site demonstrate how human civilization flourished there as long ago as the late Neolithic and Bronze Ages.

"Yi Yi Ge" Dagger

Unearthed in Nanping, Zhuhai, it is the only one of its kind found in the Pearl River estuary. This half-sword craftsmanship was most developed in China's Yunnan Province and across Vietnam. Made during the Warring States period, this find reinforces the historical connection between the Pearl River Delta and China's southwest.

"Made by Zhushi"

The style of the inscription "Zhushi suozhi", found around Shiyong Bay near Wailingding Island indicates that this original earthen jar was made during the Western Han Dynasty (206BC-24AD). This piece is the earliest cultural relic bearing Chinese characters found in the Pearl River estuary.

"GAI HUN TAN"

This eerily-shaped, elaborately designed earthen piece was used as an urn or for storing other funerary objects in cremation during the Tang and Song dynasties.

IRON PAN

In 1279, Mongol forces launched a large scale naval offensive against Song forces at Mount Ya (present-day Yamen), forcing Emperor Huizong to flee. During the ensuing Battle of Yamen on March 19, 1279, the entire Song army and navy were wiped out. The weapons, items from the daily life of soldiers and large amounts of copper coins found at the Shuijingkou site in Pingsha are important evidence of this bloody ending of a major dynasty in the history of China.

CELADON TRAY WITH FISH PATTERN

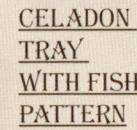

The high artistry of this piece reflects the flourishing ceramic industry of Song times in China.

TONG SHAO-YI'S ENVOY MEDAL

In 1904, Tong Shao-yi was appointed Special Commissioner to Tibet. He also visited India as China's envoy in order to negotiate the Tibet Convention, which was subsequently completed in Peking during April of 1906.

YINGYU JIQUAN 1862

Yingyu Jiquan (Chinese-English Instruction Manual), known as the earliest bilingual dictionary of spoken English and Chinese, created by Tong King-sing (1832-1892) in 1862. An influential figure in the national industrialization of China during the late Qing Dynasty (1644-1912), Tong was born in today's Zhuhai. In 1861-63, he worked with the Jardine Matheson Company in Tianjin.

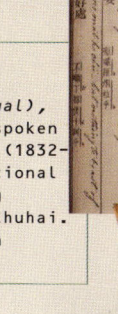

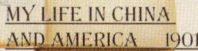

MY LIFE IN CHINA AND AMERICA 1901

The first edition of *My Life in China and America*, written by Yung Wing in 1901. Born in Nanping Village in today's Nanping Town, Zhuhai, Yung Wing was the first Chinese student known to graduate from an American university (Yale College in 1854). An early and influential figure in building relationships between China and the United States in business, education and many other fields, he brought students from China to study in the United States on the Chinese Educational Mission.

"Full Powers" Seal 1919

The seal, made of ivory, was used by Tong Shao-yi during the Shanghai peace talks between the Beiyang Warlords and the South in 1919.

Cliff Inscriptions

Located on Shixi Hill (formerly known as Songbai Hill) on the northern side of Shanchang Village in Xiangzhou District, Shixi is home to the largest cliff inscription site in Zhuhai. The rock calligraphy here was left by a good number of well-known men of letters in the Qing Dynasty (1644-1912).

QIANSHAN CITY WALL IN QIANSHAN

Started in the first year of the Tianqi reign in the Ming Dynasty (1368-1644) and expanded exclusively for military use in 1717 during Emperor Kangxi's reign in the Qing Dynasty (1644-1912).

Tong Shao-yi's Medal 1908

In 1908, the U.S Congress passed a bill to return to China the excess of Boxer Indemnity payments, amounting to over 17 million dollars. In December, Tong Shao-yi was sent by the Qing government as a special envoy to handle the issue in eight countries. The medal was awarded to him by the French government.

Tangjiawan / Doumen / Huitong Village

A STROLL into the PAST

The Tangjiawan area is an ideal place to enjoy the vibrant and rich city life in a profoundly cultural way. Beyond the famous "must-see" landmarks like Tong Shao-yi's Gongle Yuan ("Paradise for All") and his former residence, there's much more that meets the eye and satisfies the soul. It only takes a leisurely walk through the nooks and crannies for all these well-kept secrets to reveal themselves.

When your travel-worn feet enter Huitong Village, you will be in an off-road territory that makes your "journey to the west" ten-fold rewarding.

Westward from the coast and into a more bucolic area, Doumen is home to the city's most distinguished folk singers, performers, and craftsmen, and boasts an ancient street where one can sense a magnificent chapter in the history of Zhuhai.

山房路
Shanfang Road Promenade

Tongjiowan

"*Ta*^{ngjiawan}" *is, nevertheless, a somewhat misleading reference. It can refer to Tangjiawan Town, located in northern Zhuhai and in the city's "High-tech Zone". It can also refer to the village bearing the same name. However, the geographical definition of "Tangjiawan" is overshadowed by its cultural content. "Tangjiawan" plays an important, if hidden, role in the cultural landscape of Zhuhai. The birthplace of a galaxy of illustrious individuals who changed the historical routes of modern China, today's Tangjiawan is drawing new inspiration from the city's ambitious economic and educational development, and is experiencing a popularity boom.*

The cultural riches of Tangjiawan in a Chinese stamp issued in 2013

IN THE LATE QING TIMES AND EARLY YEARS OF THE REPUBLICAN PERIOD OF CHINA, MAIL SENT TO TANGJIA REQUIRED NO ADDRESS; JUST THE NAME WAS ENOUGH TO ENSURE ITS DELIVERY.

Former Residence of Tong Shao-yi

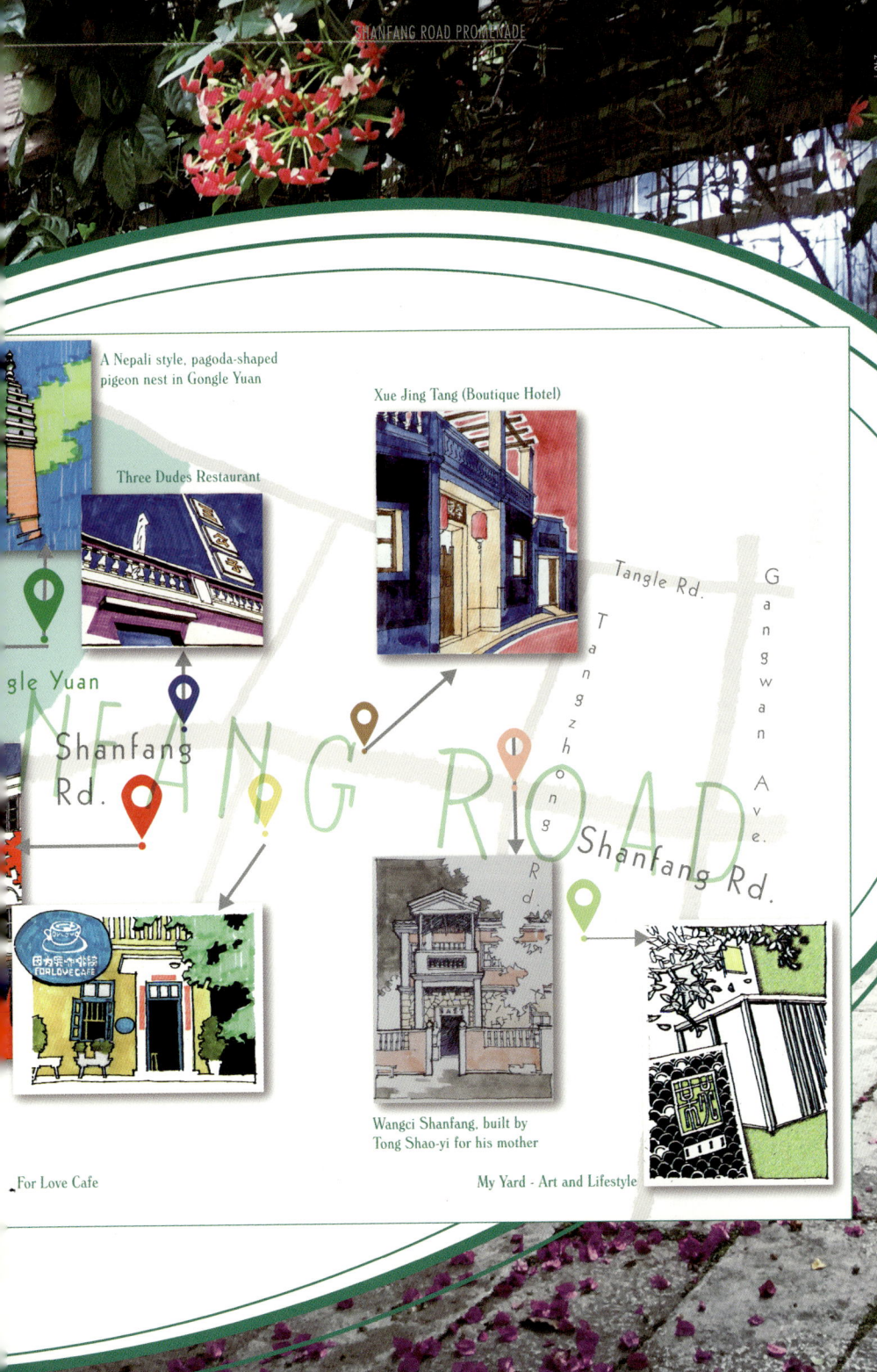

Shanfang Road, or Shanfang neighborhood, is a must-visit for any cultural traveler. Justifiably one of the city's chicest neighborhoods, Shanfang Road is a vignette of the city's cultural elegance and pride, brought alive and showcased in the texture of 21st century urban life.

Traversing historical Tangjiawan Town, the road and its labyrinth of backstreets, accessible only by foot, are strewn with cultural "gems" that make the 1.5km stretch a vibrant rendezvous for young urban professionals and a hot tourist destination. While it retains a traditional Lingnan residential atmosphere, the road now has a growing expatriate presence with a foreign business community living in the area, attracted to the privileged location of the neighborhood. Shanfang Road also has Zhuhai's largest concentration of fine bookstores, artsy eateries, bakeries and coffee shops, and holds a lively program of cultural events.

The best way to experience the charming neighborhood is setting off from the east end near Gangwan Avenue on foot. The promenade begins in the athletic, fun-loving atmosphere created by a raft of barbecue booths and confectionaries frequented by students from nearby Zhuhai Campus of Sun Yat-sen University. The noise and excitement fades into tranquility as you walk the outer reaches of the road, like walking away from modern times into a simpler, slower life. Crowds are smaller, lines are shorter, and coffeehouse staff and pastry chefs have plenty of time to show off their products.

This charming spell grows stronger and reaches its peak about 500 meters into the 1,500-meter passage, when

SHANFANG ROAD PROMENADE

The unassuming front of For Love Cafe, a household name among the city's coffee lovers

you bump into the red brick façade of Wangci Shanfang, built by Tong Shao-yi for his mother, and providing the name of the road. In late Qing times and the early years of the Republican Period, mail sent to Tangjia required no address—just the name was enough to ensure its delivery to this unmistakable spot. Today, the dust on the Tangjiawan Post Office has been wiped away, but the significance of the refurbished building may be easy to miss in the hurried glances of tourists. However, it is in this humble corner that the historical eminence of Tangjiawan rears its proud head.

Walking further into the road's maze of bifurcations, you will be in an exhilarating wonderland of architectural attractions with a smorgasbord of boutique shops, stylish hostels and eateries, more than sufficiently photogenic for crafting another *In the Mood for Love* by Wong Kar-wai. Be

SHANFANG ROAD PROMENADE

warned: don't get so lost in déjà vu that you can't make it back to reality.

The road then tapers down near the enclosing walls of Tong's remaining estate. Situated on the highest terrain in Tangjia Village, Tong Shao-yi's former residence leads you into a world of refreshing solemnity, purified by thrushes singing their hearts out.

Alternatively, head all the way from the west tip, where the grandiose, operatic garden of the most remembered resident of Tangjiawan presents itself to you. A petite temple nestles nearby, deeply shaded under the age-old banyan tree. From the contented faces of the locals whiling away lazy afternoons in the lovely yard carpeted with delicate, rosy petals, one can be forgiven in making the assumption that the road's humble inhabitants somehow take their privileged residence for granted.

East and west, Home is the best.

A Paradise For All

Regarded as one of the "top three private gardens" in today's Zhuhai, this elaborately built garden is an architectural treasure that reflects both Tong Shao-yi's highly developed aesthetics fostered by the man's Chinese roots and the western part of his soul.

Hidden beneath layers of indigenous, exuberant flora nourished by the ample rain and constant humidity of southern China are thick smears of historical heaviness and solemnity. Tong's garden is a "hard" one that defies all the soft, feminine clichés of traditional, "Jiangnan style" garden landscaping. The gnarled branches of the banyan trees seem to have been there since remote times, presenting a vista that reminds the visitor of the fantastical Wizarding World of Harry Potter. The aisle columns that have watched a century tumultuously roll by still glisten with the tantalizing luster of an oyster. The man's untamed soul is embodied in the lavish and wild beauty of this timeless retreat, presenting the mystery of a "Garden of Eden", and making it truly one-of-its-kind in China's "Lingnan" region.

East and west, home is the best.

At the age of 48, a disillusioned Tong Shao-yi had lost all interest in making waves in the flashy and ostentatious masquerade of high-stakes business ventures. By that time, he had lived a full life of wealth and fame, making many friends as well as enemies. In 1910, the 48-year-old Tong went home to build a garden he fondly named "Exquisite Yamadate" (literally "Exquisite Mountain House"). His homesickness at that time ran so wild and joy of return so deep that he planted five-hundred litchi trees in the sprawling garden, in some attempt to regain the "taste of home". In the heat of mid-summer, Tong Shao-yi enjoyed the company of his like-minded friends and spent long days playing chess with the villagers under the wisteria arbor, the seasonal revelry bringing him immense solace.

Tong Shao-yi built a Nepali style, pagoda-shaped pigeon nest in the garden, praying for the message of peace to be brought back by his avian friends.

A PARADISE FOR ALL

The garden is not only a botanical wonderland with a dazzling collection of exotic plants, but also a private "gym" fully equipped with a hard surface tennis court and a stairway that requires quite a climb. The stairway collapsed in a rainstorm in 1938, with 76 of the original 100 steps remaining to this day. Perhaps it's no coincidence that Tong Shao-yi lived to be 67.

Tong Shao-yi renamed the garden as the "Paradise for All" in 1921, the year he officially retired from the world to indulge his lifetime fascination with plants. Like a cicada sloughing off its skin in spring, the armor on Tong Shao-yi was taken off, with the hedonist and green thumb in him finally regaining dominance. Now the man became the ruler of his own "Elysium", where admission is believed to have been reserved for mortals chosen by the gods. Tong Shao-yi gave one of the reservations in this "Elysium" to his friend and colleague, Herbert Clark Hoover, the 31st President of the United States (from 1929 to 1933 during the Great Depression). "It was a beautiful Southern-China style vacation that we spent in Tong's private garden in his hometown," Hoover reminisced in his memoir. Obviously, the garden's "greenhouse", with a lovely fireplace, was designed based on Tong's memory of where

The garden's observatory, a two-story structure equipped with a sextant, was the only one of its kind in China at the time when it was constructed.

he lived during his American years and naturally made the former president feel pleasantly dry and cozy in the hot and muggy climate of southern China.

The garden's other distinguished guests also included Edgar Snow and Mei Lanfang, who planted a "beauty tree" here during his visit in 1931.

The garden's observatory, a two-story structure equipped with a sextant, was the only one of its kind in China at the time when it was constructed, and must have taken the interplay of a western-influenced mind and soaring, adventurous spirit to include such a sci-fi element. It is not hard for the more sensitive among us to imagine how Tong Shao-yi preserved his sanity by steering his gaze and thoughts away from precarious political circles and fickle human relationship towards the starry sky for the ultimate answers.

Throughout his life, Tong Shao-yi never abandoned his dream of making the world a better place for all people to share. The seed of world peace was probably sown in him in his teens by the Old Testament story of Noah's ark. Seeing people suffer

Tong's homesickness at that time ran so wild and joy of return so deep that he planted five-hundred litchi trees in the sprawling garden, in some attempt to regain the "taste of home".

always tormented him as well. He built a Nepali style, pagoda-shaped pigeon nest in the garden, praying for the message of peace to be brought back by his avian friends.

Tong donated the lavish garden to his home village in 1932, making it "a paradise for all" as the name suggests. The inscription of the garden's new name on the entrance arch is in the original handwriting of Tong.

If Fan Zhongyan (989-1052), a founder of Neo-Confucianism and a great statesman of the Northern Song Dynasty (960-1279), lived up to what he preached: "Be the first to bear the world's hardship, and the last to enjoy its comfort", then Tong Shao-yi brought Fan's ideal to a new realm in which he shared the world's comfort and beauty with all people.

In the old times, Qianshan River was the shared "mother river" of today's Zhuhai and Macao, on the southern shore of which lies a quiet settlement called Beishan. Most of the dwellings in the old village area face north, which is reputedly a testament to the patriotism and unflinching loyalty of a legendary military family whose unmatched gallantry and sacrifice comprised a saga of heroism.

A Family Above and Beyond

Beishan Village

It is widely believed that today's residents of Beishan are the progeny of the Yang family generals, known for their unflinching loyalty and remarkable bravery as they sacrificed themselves to defend the country from foreign military powers. It is believed that a score of survivors of the Yang lineage wound up in this "end of the earth" either in the Yuanfeng years of the Northern Song period or later during the Jiaxi reign of the Southern Song. The Yang clan reached its zenith in the Qing Dynasty, leaving its spectral and haunting allure in the village's many elaborately built ancestral temples and running through a long list of local legends.

Representing the architectural style of the prosperous, middle-class of "Lingnan" (southern China) and itself the largest in the Zhuhai territory, the Yang Clan Ancestral Hall is the sweet home of the famous "harbinger of spring"—four, hundred-year-old magnolia trees. When in bloom, the message of springtime is sent to every corner of Zhuhai. Rumor has it that the trees were purchased from the Jiangnan region (to the north, but south of the Yangtze River) by the Yang family in 1828, more for the comforting memory of their roots in the Central China Plain than as a badge of their family glory.

First built in 1868, the lavish building is decked out in two parts, divided by a pair of stone lions, covered with artful flourishes and numerous exquisite details that show the military bearing of the family. The most striking features of the complex are authentic, Lingnan-style carvings, matching perfectly with the overall design. When the sun blasts down on the secluded courtyard, the porcelain window lattices glisten with mesmerizing cobalt blue that rivals the luster of a sapphire. It is easy to imagine what a fine place this would have been to live in back in those days.

The long list of village legends includes Yang Zhenhai (1828-1903), a division commander in the late Qing period, and the son of Yang Yunxiang (1801-1872), whose bravery repelled the British invaders and impressed Emperor Xianfeng.

A very special contributor of the time-honored glory of Beishan is Yang Pao'an (1896-1931), a Chinese Communist pioneer and the author of *A Brief History of the West*, China's first systematic recounting of the history of the international communist movement.

(Go to "Chapter 7" for more about the charming neighborhood of Beishan.)

rising wind and flying clouds

Huitong Village

During the Yongzheng reign of the Qing Dynasty, at the end of the 18th and beginning of 19th centuries, an affable country gentleman named Mok Yue-king (Mo Yujing), settled down with a close circle of friends in an attractive but previously unoccupied part of present-day Zhuhai that came to be known as "Huitong Village". Being the very first to appreciate and devote themselves to this "land of promise", the village's first three families, named Mok, Bao and Ouyang, thrived and continued as the leading influence.

Being a sincere and selfless community leader, Mok Yue-king continued to receive the respect and trust of the villagers, attracting more people to settle there as word spread. Ancestral homes were built, and the Mok family grew to be the biggest and most powerful clan in the village that was later named after Mok Yue-king's other "literary" name—"Huitong". The Mok family flourished famously over time, culminating in its "Taikoo era", a glorious period of 61 years in which three generations of men in the Mok lineage achieved stellar careers at Taikoo Sugar Refinery, the largest operation in Hong Kong, which was run by the Swire Group, a London-headquartered conglomerate with enormous resources. In the space of one century, almost 1,000 members of the Mok clan worked with Taikoo. Some sources claim that the influence of the single family was so great, in fact, that it led at last to a shake-up and the resignation of Mok Kon-sang (1882-1958) in 1931.

Thanks to the extensively connected and well-informed Mok family, and its community spirit, the

A Family Above and Beyond

Beishan Village

It is widely believed that today's residents of Beishan are the progeny of the Yang family generals, known for their unflinching loyalty and remarkable bravery as they sacrificed themselves to defend the country from foreign military powers. It is believed that a score of survivors of the Yang lineage wound up in this "end of the earth" either in the Yuanfeng years of the Northern Song period or later during the Jiaxi reign of the Southern Song. The Yang clan reached its zenith in the Qing Dynasty, leaving its spectral and haunting allure in the village's many elaborately built ancestral temples and running through a long list of local legends.

Representing the architectural style of the prosperous, middle-class of "Lingnan" (southern China) and itself the largest in the Zhuhai territory, the Yang Clan Ancestral Hall is the sweet home of the famous "harbinger of spring"—four, hundred-year-old magnolia trees. When in bloom, the message of springtime is sent to every corner of Zhuhai. Rumor has it that the trees were purchased from the Jiangnan region (to the north, but south of the Yangtze River) by the Yang family in 1828, more for the comforting memory of their roots in the Central China Plain than as a badge of their family glory.

First built in 1868, the lavish building is decked out in two parts, divided by a pair of stone lions, covered with artful flourishes and numerous exquisite details that show the military bearing of the family. The most striking features of the complex are authentic, Lingnan-style carvings, matching perfectly with the overall design. When the sun blasts down on the secluded courtyard, the porcelain window lattices glisten with mesmerizing cobalt blue that rivals the luster of a sapphire. It is easy to imagine what a fine place this would have been to live in back in those days.

The long list of village legends includes Yang Zhenhai (1828-1903), a division commander in the late Qing period, and the son of Yang Yunxiang (1801-1872), whose bravery repelled the British invaders and impressed Emperor Xianfeng.

A very special contributor of the time-honored glory of Beishan is Yang Pao'an (1896-1931), a Chinese Communist pioneer and the author of *A Brief History of the West*, China's first systematic recounting of the history of the international communist movement. (Go to "Chapter 7" for more about the charming neighborhood of Beishan.)

A FAMILY ABOVE AND BEYOND

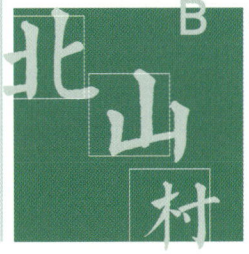

Beishan

北
山
村

When the sun
blasts down on
the secluded
courtyard, the
porcelain window
lattices glisten
with mesmerizing
cobalt blue that
rivals the luster
of a sapphire.

rising wind and flying clouds

Huitong Village

During the Yongzheng reign of the Qing Dynasty, at the end of the 18th and beginning of 19th centuries, an affable country gentleman named Mok Yue-king (Mo Yujing), settled down with a close circle of friends in an attractive but previously unoccupied part of present-day Zhuhai that came to be known as "Huitong Village". Being the very first to appreciate and devote themselves to this "land of promise", the village's first three families, named Mok, Bao and Ouyang, thrived and continued as the leading influence.

Being a sincere and selfless community leader, Mok Yue-king continued to receive the respect and trust of the villagers, attracting more people to settle there as word spread. Ancestral homes were built, and the Mok family grew to be the biggest and most powerful clan in the village that was later named after Mok Yue-king's other "literary" name—"Huitong". The Mok family flourished famously over time, culminating in its "Taikoo era", a glorious period of 61 years in which three generations of men in the Mok lineage achieved stellar careers at Taikoo Sugar Refinery, the largest operation in Hong Kong, which was run by the Swire Group, a London-headquartered conglomerate with enormous resources. In the space of one century, almost 1,000 members of the Mok clan worked with Taikoo. Some sources claim that the influence of the single family was so great, in fact, that it led at last to a shake-up and the resignation of Mok Kon-sang (1882-1958) in 1931.

Thanks to the extensively connected and well-informed Mok family, and its community spirit, the

villagers here were the first in Guangdong Province to enjoy the modern luxury of electricity, tap water and motion pictures. Indeed, the accepted view among historians is that this village was the first one in China to reach modernity at a time when the rest of China was struggling to catch up.

Over the course of some 200 years, the settlement of Huitong thrived and developed into a typically Lingnan-style residential hive, with this supportive environment becoming home to a host of business dignitaries and esteemed officials. These days there aren't many dignitaries around—there aren't many people around—but those who do still call Huitong their home are members of a lucky bunch in many ways.

Despite its proven history of notable glory and two bustling modern university campuses just a stone's throw away, the village today is largely untouched by the constantly modernizing world around it and spared stampeding shoppers and tourists. It feels like it has been simply left to its own devices, as an island in time; the quiet lanes and withering facades only serve to compound this sense of genuine antiquity.

The beauty of this quiet settlement is a raw kind—honest and straightforward, but all the better for it.

Separated from the outside by rammed-earth walls, the village features a chessboard-type layout that draws on the principles of Western village design. The most striking buildings in this blessed settlement include two western-style watchtowers: the one in the north bearing the inscription, "Rising Wind", and the other in the south, "Flying Clouds". The stunningly well-preserved ancestral temples of the Mok clan are lined up imposingly in the most prominent part of the village. Behind the temples are more than 40 residential buildings with artful flourishes filling every corner and bringing elegance to the overall design and impression given to passersby.

The most striking buildings in this blessed settlement include two western-style watchtowers: the one in the north bearing the inscription, "Rising Wind", and the other in the south, "Flying Clouds".

Cool, dark, and quiet, with an abundance of whispers from the past to keep you company, one need not be inclined to melancholia to appreciate the coffee house in the romantically tragic Qixia Xianguan residence. With languorous walkways leading through sleepy courtyards, a visitor may be quite content wandering past lush Longan trees, examining the beautiful tile work below or architecture above, both difficult to categorize owing to the diverse styles the creators drew from. If you crave human company or mental stimulation, however, you can find a bustling scene in the cafes and restaurants neatly situated in the village's many old residences or drop in to the Readzone Bookstore set in one of the village's ancestral temples that were built by the Mok family. Leaving the village, walking across unusually luxurious lawns and past one of the distinctive watchtowers, one might have the feeling of awakening from a dream had long ago.

Forever Apart, Always Together

Qixia Xianguan: An ethereal place where the sunset glow perches

The most eloquent and touching expression of Huitong Village's mystique is the "Wuthering Heights of Zhuhai", haunting, romantic and brooding—tucked away in the village's southeast corner. Walking into the mansion, residing there like some frazzled hermit, puts one in mind of Emily Bronte's snowed-in farmhouse on the moors in 1801, with all its creepy secrets.

栖霞仙館

FOREVER APART, ALWAYS TOGETHER

Qixia Xianguan was used as the main shooting site for the 2014 thriller *Death Ouija*, starring Hong Kong actor Fang Lishen.

Qixia Xianguan (literally "Ethereal Dwelling Where the Sunset Glow Perches"), was built by Mok Ying Chow (Mo Yongyu), the grandson of Mok See Yong (Mo Shiyang), in memory of his first wife and only true love. Affectionately called "A Xia" (the second character meaning "sunset glow"), she was a beautiful lady who received her education in Japan. Her posthumous memorial is now one of the top three garden attractions in Zhuhai, undoubtedly also the most romantic, yet in a tragic way.

The loving man's wistful sentiments are dust-sealed in the centerpiece of the garden— a painstakingly decorated, 400-square-meter, arcaded "dwelling" that combines Chinese, Japanese and Southeast Asian architectural elements. All construction materials were imported from Hong Kong and beyond, with the stylish floor tiles imported directly from Italy. The care and expense that the devoted, mourning husband lavished on immortalizing his beloved is reminiscent of other monuments to lost love, like the Taj Mahal, that share a spiritual bond. Decked out on two floors, the structure originally included a sutra hall, where resident nuns chanted in hope of releasing the soul of A Xia from purgatory.

After marrying his beautiful sweetheart, Mok Ying Chow considered himself the luckiest man in the world, but the two love-birds were not destined to a long life of wedded bliss. At the age of only 30, A Xia died of an illness. The devastated Mok Ying Chow spent more than 1,000 silver taels building her the perfect home, but one she would never set foot in and, with its shadow of her premature death, one he could never truly depart. Lovers today, visiting the garden, can easily imagine a bereft and despondent Mok Ying Chow sitting in the Japanese-style cottage alone in silence, eyes brimming with sorrowful tears, fragile heart broken, and drinking the bitter wine of lost love to the bottom.

The garden has an Indian-style Litchi Lounge, where the elegant lady must have whiled away many dreamy, mid-summer afternoons, savoring the seasonal treat and cuddling with her man. The garden's gate tower is also a bell-house, but the bell is nowhere to be found, just like the mansion's ghostly hostess and the other secrets that have eluded researchers.

The litchi trees have grown bigger, but all else has turned to dust. The yard is a botanical wonderland of rare plant species running riot to create a rain-forest scene, fueled perhaps by the unspent passion of the star-crossed lovers.

Today, a coffeehouse on the second floor of the residence is ideal for the love-stricken and nostalgic to admire the soulful romance and envision a beautiful, contented A Xia coming home at last.

The untamed greenery that presents a dreamlike vista and the façade decaying with dignity over the vicissitudes of time, together with the dilapidated gateway, render the memorial yard eerily beautiful.

Legend of Doumen

斗門墟

In the eyes of many, Zhuhai is all about youthful charm—beautiful scenery combined with the vigor of modernity. And yet, coastline vistas and impressive infrastructure represent only one of the many wonderful aspects of the area and, traveling to the west, the city gives way to secrets seemingly lost in time, encountering intriguing names like "Knife-sharpening Gate" and "Tiger's Run Passage".

A Breathing Time-capsule

John C. Young (1912-1987)

Doumen is the home of the Zhaozhen Museum, named after U.S. Army Colonel, John C. Young (Rong Zhaozhen), whose father was born near here.

A Chinese American born in San Jose, California, John C. Young was a key figure in the development of San Francisco's Chinatown, and a decorated American World War II army veteran of the China-Myanmar-India theater. He was celebrated as one of the 20 individuals from San Francisco history "who was heroic in stature and contributed significantly to the building of the San Francisco we know today".

John was the second son of Young Soong Quong (Rong Songguang), who was born in Longtan Village, located to the north of Jing'an Town in today's Doumen. Young Soong Quong went to America at the age of 11 and became a resident of California, with John later growing up in San Jose's Chinatown. He retired as a reserve officer in 1972 with the rank of full colonel. The Engineer from Stanford University cherished his Chinese roots so much that he devoted his later years to the improvement of San Francisco's Chinatown and helped found the annual Chinese New Year's Parade. John was remembered by people in his ancestral home as the first Chinese to be awarded the rank of colonel during World War II. But, for the people of San Francisco, the man was loved most as the co-founder of the first factory in the United States that manufactured soy sauce using the old Chinese fermentation process.

Col. Young and his wife Mary Lee (Li Ruxin) donated their extensive collection of Chinese imperial robes and Chinese jade to the Stanford University Cantor Center for Visual Arts and to the Tacoma Art Museum. Shortly after Col. Young's death, Mary funded the building of a museum near Young's father's ancestral village.

Originally part of the territory of Zhongshan and Xinhui areas, Doumen officially joined the jurisdictional domain of Zhuhai as late as 1983 as a county and became one of the city's core districts in 2001.

Long ago, the current location of Doumen was within a bay area cut into halves by the rugged Huangyang Mountain range and constantly reshaped by the surrounding rivers, flowing to the South China Sea and forming the Pearl River Delta. With its pivotal location in terms of water transportation, the thousand-year prosperity of Doumen is a perfect illustration of the way in which the confluence of rivers can result in a land of cornucopia.

Called Doumen "Xu"(in Chinese "xu" 墟 meaning "ruins" but also, as in this case, "market" or "bazaar"), the old town area that sits at the southern tip of the Pearl River Delta served as the "west conduit" of Zhuhai throughout its history. The archaic name alone is a good indicator of the historical remoteness of this intriguing artifact of a town, left behind in time as the rest of the area developed and modernized.

The centerpiece of Doumen Xu is a business street that thrived throughout the mid-19th century into the early years of the 20th century, thanks to the bustling trade and cultural interaction between local businesspeople, and dealers and missionaries from Macao, Europe, North America and other areas.

Col. John C. Young and Mary Lee Young, a San Francisco-born Chinese-American

OLD TALES & SECRETS

DOUMEN OLD STREET

斗門舊街

Beating Heart of Doumen "Market"

While it is true that many towns and cities across China, especially in the southern parts of the country, have their own "old streets"—bustling thoroughfares where you can experience life as it used to be— Zhuhai's handful of ancient towns and villages really stand out, with the Doumen Old Street—the town's centerpiece— being a distinctive landmark, not only for the city's Doumen District but also the greater Zhuhai area.

LEGEND OF DOUMEN

In its heyday in the late 19th century, architects and churchmen from Hong Kong, Macao, Europe and North America came here, and many of them settled in this bustling place packed with a range of business and services including money houses handling foreign exchange services.

The ancient street nestled in the beating heart of the Doumen "Xu" is not merely a spruced up, gaudy street under the guise of "authenticity". The booths are not just ghostly shells of the past, but are still quite lived-in. Despite its small population, this exquisitely decaying monument is still breathing, with well-conserved southern China style arcade buildings, attracting film crews throughout the year. This seemingly sleepy hamlet routinely comes alive when the local leadership puts on its cultural festival, called by the locals as "*xu ri*" and still energetically celebrated by today's townspeople.

Veering off the shopfront corridor into the rear of this intricate urban structure, one is led to a lovely, still occupied quarter, once permeated with family happiness and still blessed with the fragrance of fruit trees. Walking under t window lattices now feels pleasantly anachronistic. Elderly women fan themselves as they chitchat with neighbors, and dogs laze about on the pavement occasionally peeking at the passersby. The locals' laundry gently moves in the breeze as it hangs drying, draped over the beams, and you just cannot resist the temptation to peer into someone's dimly lit home as an elderly man sits still as a statue staring back at you.

Towards the outskirts of the

old town, bright yellow roof tiles contrast against imposing white apartments, marking the end of the walled-in sample of a lifestyle gone by.

In its heyday in the late 19th century, architects and churchmen from Hong Kong, Macao, Europe and North America poured into this "land of plenty", many of them settling down in the bustling enclave packed with an extensive mix of business and services. The result was a 500-meter stretch (designed by Canadian engineer Rev. John Galloway), elaborately decorated with a bold combination of Southeast Asian and Southern Chinese elements, creating the perfect setting for the coming-and-goings of foreign visitors and ne'er-do-wells alike, interacting with local groceries, TCM drugstores, rice shops, fabric dealers, pawn shops and money houses handling foreign exchange services. The vivid scenes and intense interaction witnessed in the bustling past of this street is hard to imagine today.

In the late 18th century, the area went through reconstruction during the reign of Qianlong, enjoying increasing prosperity through the Republican Era and beyond, but eventually slowing down as fortunes shifted with the transition of the city's economic hub in the late 20th century. The street's dizzying colors and the town's glory became dust-laden, but visitors today can still sense its former brilliance. The irony is that, probably because of its "natural phase-out", the street became the only survivor amidst gentrification in the old street heritage of Zhuhai. The fortunate result is that, with a little imagination, as you stroll along the withering arcades, through a plethora of shady courtyards, admiring exquisite flourishes, you can still relive the noise, the loud baby cries and laughter, that was once here.

The result was a 500-meter stretch creating the perfect setting for the coming-and-goings of foreign visitors and ne'er-do-wells alike.

菜 猗 堂

SHELL-PROOF

Luyi Tang

Whether the shell walls are bulletproof is unknown, but the stunningly well-conserved facade obviously has survived numerous typhoons in a space of more than 600 years. The baptism of time only adds luster to the mythical elegance of the houses, presenting magical interaction between natural gifts and human ingenuity.

A kilometer or so west of the elegant "bazaar" of Doumen, one can trace its legend back to Zhao Kuangying (927-976), the founder and first emperor of the Song Dynasty (960-1279), in the sun-drenched courtyards of Luyi Tang—a stately ancestral temple complex—and gain fresh perspectives on Doumen's daunting historical record, as well as the wider "Lingnan" area.

As the widely accepted story goes, it was in Yamen (today's Yamen Town of Xinhui City) that Wen Tianxiang (1236-1283) was written into the history of the Song. It is here that he fought and lost his last battles, refusing to yield to the Yuan invaders; and that the Zhao-surnamed villagers living in the nearby Nanmen Village vainly risked their lives to save the Song royal lineage from extermination.

It was in this isolated "gate on the sea" that the Song empire walked into an impasse in the death struggle and met its doom. The sea battle, seen by historians as a rarity in the history of ancient China, witnessed the tragic death of 44-year-old Prime Minister Lu Xiufu (1236-1279), carrying the young Emperor, Zhao Bing, and jumping into the

sea. The yearnings of the man's unfulfilled soul can still be heard by today's people emanating from the furious billows. It is also believed that the survivors found refuge in the depths of Huangyang Mountain and built a cottage that evolved into today's Jintai Temple, another cultural gem in Doumen.

Genealogical studies show the royal blood of Nanmen Village sprang from Zhao Yifu, an 8th-generation descendant of Zhao Kuangmei (a younger brother of Zhao Kuangying), 29 years before the bloody battle that sent Wen Tianxiang into four years of purgatory suffering in the military prison of the Yuan. Zhao Yifu landed in today's Zhuhai to swear in as the county magistrate in the year 1234. In the course of the next 700 years, the Zhao clan thrived for more than 30 generations, all taking great pride in their ancestral

In 1454, Zhao Meinan's great-grandson built an ancestral hall and named it using characters taken from one of his great-grandfather's honorific titles. The name, "Luyi Tang", means "Hall of Exuberance".

roots. The traditional Song value of "loyalty" was so deep-rooted in the Zhao's family tree that it remained strong in Zhao Meinan (1296-1365), belonging to the fourth generation of Zhao Yifu's descendants, who lived in seclusion, avoiding officialdom his entire life, writing books and tending bamboo groves. In 1454, his great-grandson built an ancestral hall and named it using characters taken from the literary name of his great-grandfather. The name, "Luyi Tang", means "Hall of Exuberance".

It does not take an eagle-eyed visitor to notice the unusual architectural details dotted around the complex that is divided into three parts by courtyards. The intricate layout and the many fine details throughout make the ancestral building an open-air southern China sculpture museum. For today's people, the most awe-inspiring feature of the building is its walls, measuring about 65 centimeters in thickness and made of layers of oyster shells. The tradition of using the shells as a construction material started from the Ming Dynasty (1368-1644). Whether the shell walls are bulletproof is unknown, but the stunningly well-conserved façade obviously has survived numerous typhoons in a space of more than 600 years. The baptism of time only adds luster to the mythical elegance of the houses, presenting magical interaction between natural gifts and human ingenuity.

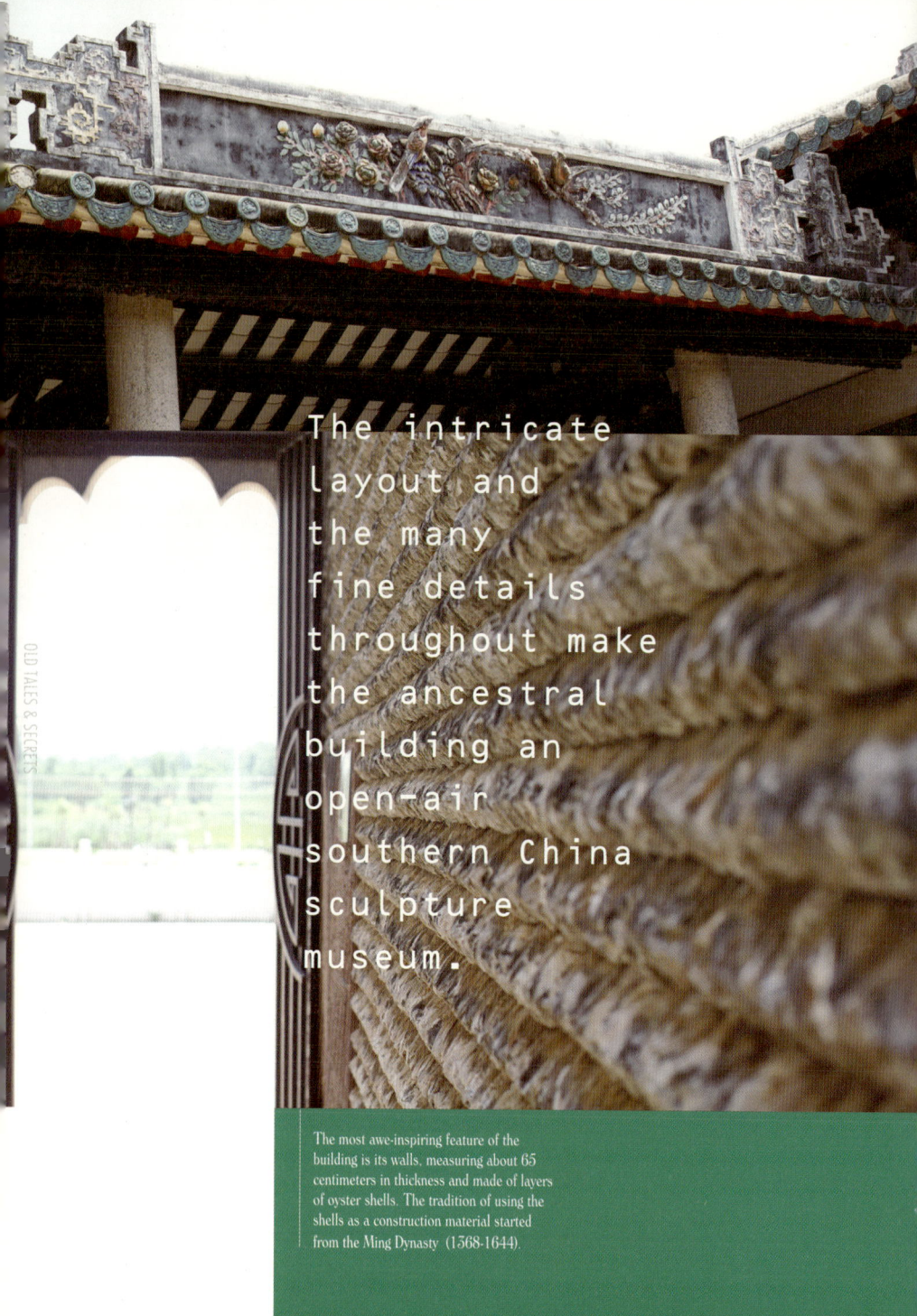

The intricate layout and the many fine details throughout make the ancestral building an open-air southern China sculpture museum.

The most awe-inspiring feature of the building is its walls, measuring about 65 centimeters in thickness and made of layers of oyster shells. The tradition of using the shells as a construction material started from the Ming Dynasty (1368-1644).

SHELL-PROOF

Jintai Temple

700 Years of Solitude and Solemnity

金臺寺

For more of the most authentic historical sights and sensations in weather-worn Doumen, the district's peripheral blocks are strewn with cultural spots that ensure a rewarding experience.

The birthplace of the city's many cultural notables, folk arts and crafts, Doumen now hosts six of the "top eight attractions of Doumen District", including Zhuhai's best hot spring resort built on a daily yield of hot spring water reaching 2,400 tons and an average temperature gauged at 68℃-70℃, Huangyang Mountain—the "number one peak in the Pearl Delta", and the Jintai Temple, first built approximately 700 years ago.

The vicissitudes of Doumen have been mirrored by the Jintai Temple. First built approximately 700 years ago by the remnants of the dying Southern Song Dynasty (1127-1279), the striking building in the style of ancient times with orange-colored roof tiles is a remake of the original temple site, located deep in the south foot of Huangyang Mountain, overlooking Yamen seaport and presenting a graceful, awe-inspiring sight. On the opposite bank of the mountain is an imposing rock named "Dengxian", from which the legendary "Cowboy King" of Doumen ascended to heaven and immortality. The locals believe the soul of Zhang Shijie, one of the "three generals of the late Southern Song", rests near the temple's original site.

OLD TALES & SECRETS

> The three dwellings thrived and became known as a romantic enclave over the next 200 years.

接霞莊

JIEXIA ESTATE

"Receiving the Sunset Glow Retreat"

Not as old as Luyi Tang, but similarly mythical, Jie Xia Zhuang (Jiexia Estate) is a charming hideaway located a kilometer or so west of Luyi Tang, with a rustic allure and an origin story that should tickle the fancy of those with a sense of the supernatural. The injustice is that tourists and the younger generations of the locals tend to favor more famous scenic and cultural attractions in Doumen, making this village a whistle stop, given only a cursory glance at best or totally ignored at worst.

According to legend, the founding fathers of Jiexia Estate were Zhao Ruokun and his son Weimao, living in the Daoguang years of the Qing Dynasty (early 19th century) and building the family fortune through a TCM pharmacy business. Seeking a new place to settle down, the family chanced to find what they believed to be a private Xanadu. They built three rammed-earth houses on a clearing that nestles at the northern slope of Xiashan Hill ("Evening Glow Hill"), believing that the misty clouds whirling around the forests were an auspicious sign. The three dwellings thrived and became known as a romantic enclave over the next 200 years. The original name "Zhao's Village" gave way to a more charming moniker "Jie Xia Zhuang" ("*jie xia*" meaning, "taking in the evening glow").

An attractive and comforting feature of this primitive but soothing village is a moat-style stream, stretching around the village for 350 meters and making it a world of its own. The dwellings stand as they did hundreds of years ago and, while the ravages of time have undoubtedly taken their toll on the slumping rooftops and faded walls, the natural decline only adds to their authentic beauty.

Surveying the village's mesmerizing beauty of fine architecture and intricate landscaping, one can almost believe in the witchcraft of the mysterious clouds that fascinated the villager's ancestors in the first place. It seems that the clouds are still wielding magic today, protecting the Shangri-la from gentrification and the restless onslaught of modernity.

The cultural "pearls" of Zhuhai, strewn across the city's sparsely populated outposts and on sundrenched coasts, form a snapshot of a remarkably gifted region full of wonders and talented individuals, whose skill and unfailing passion elevates the city into the nation's folk culture "super league", breathing fire into art forms that were quickly being forgotten. From the "Crane King" Chen Fuyan, aged 85, to kung fu master Huang Buyun, unsung heroes are snatching "pearls" from the jaws of oblivion in their own humble way.

The colorful folk arts and cultural delights of Zhuhai also include the Phoenix-Rooster Dance, Awakening Lion Dance and the Fire Dragon Dance. And, if you are in Zhuhai at the right time of year, you may bump into locals busy enthralling tourists with Lingnan-style kung fu and One-Thumb Massage.

From the "Crane King" Chen Fuyan to kung fu master Huang Buyun, unsung heroes are snatching "pearls" from the jaws of oblivion in their own humble way.

THE CULTURAL PEARLS

THE CULTURAL PEARLS

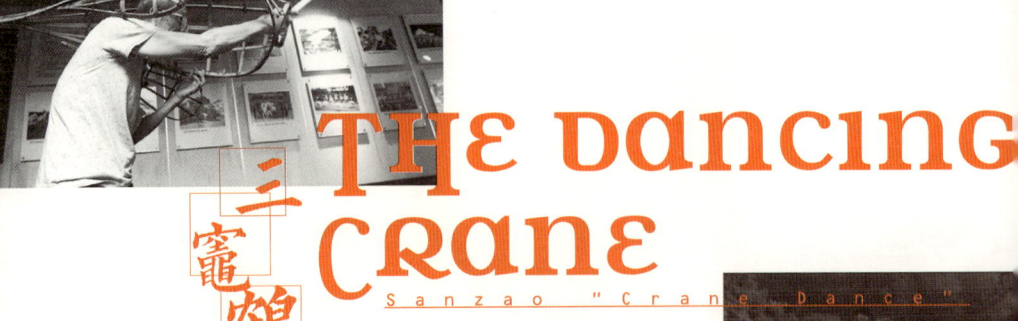

THE DANCING CRANE

三竈鶴舞

Sanzao "Crane Dance"

1997 was the most important year in the life of Deng Aizhen, born in Guangxi Zhuang Autonomous Region, and a pivotal year in the life of Chen Fuyan, living in a small village in Sanzao Town, Zhuhai. That year, a newly married Deng Aizhen settled down in Haicheng and saw the village's New Year "crane dance" for the first time in her life, without knowing she would become the first female "crane dancer" and the only female inheritor of a cultural hallmark of her adopted home. If these two persevering souls had never crossed paths, it is highly possible that the town's most treasured cultural art form, now recognized in the country's gleaming, state-level, cultural heritage "hall of fame", would have been lost forever, resigned to the dustbin of history or, at best, the dwindling memory of isolated old men to whom the world has no time to listen.

Throughout a history that dates back to Song Dynasty (960-1279), it had been an unwritten rule that the secrets of the dance, together with its crane-making craftsmanship, were to be passed exclusively to males; and rumor had it that a woman who learned the trick would be cursed and have babies with legs as lanky and frail as a crane's.

The fateful day for Deng Aizhen, who had been eking out a living as a cleaner at the Zhuhai Airport, came in 2011, when the city was bracing for the international tourism festival to be held in Guangzhou. A curious Deng, turning 40 that year, attended the qualification trials to test her luck, and caught the eye of Chen Fuyan —the "crane king" in Sanzao. The chance meeting of the two changed the course of the "Crane Dance" history, and at just the right moment.

The relay baton was finally passed to "the right person" at the very time that the tradition was teetering on the edge of cultural oblivion. The more details and secrets Deng Aizhen learned about the craft, the more spellbound she became, drawn into its unique artistry. In 2013, the former airport cleaner became the proud district-level "guardian" of this unique tradition.

OLD TALES & SECRETS

Sanzao "Crane Dance"

One of the crown jewels of Zhuhai's cultural pride, the "Crane Dance" is a dying folk art that originated in the Sanzao area of southern Zhuhai. In ancient times, the vast mangrove forests, mudflats and marsh sprawls made the islands a food paradise for fowls and beasts. The locals' "crane totem" evolved into a singing and dancing form that later became a standard program in the festival calendar of Sanzao. The dance team mimics the long-observed movements of the crane—such as foraging, preening, putting up the wing, frolicking and homing—under powerful, boisterous music and singing. Underneath the jubilant presentation is a strong current of solemnity expressed through three choreographic climaxes symbolizing the immortalization of the "cranes" ascending to heaven.

The story of Chen Fuyan, together with the intriguing "Crane Dance" tradition of Sanzao, was transformed into a short documentary directed by Li Weinian, who is also an avid advocate of the protection of Zhuhai's cultural relics. In the film, the octogenarian made his cinematic debut by playing the "crane king".

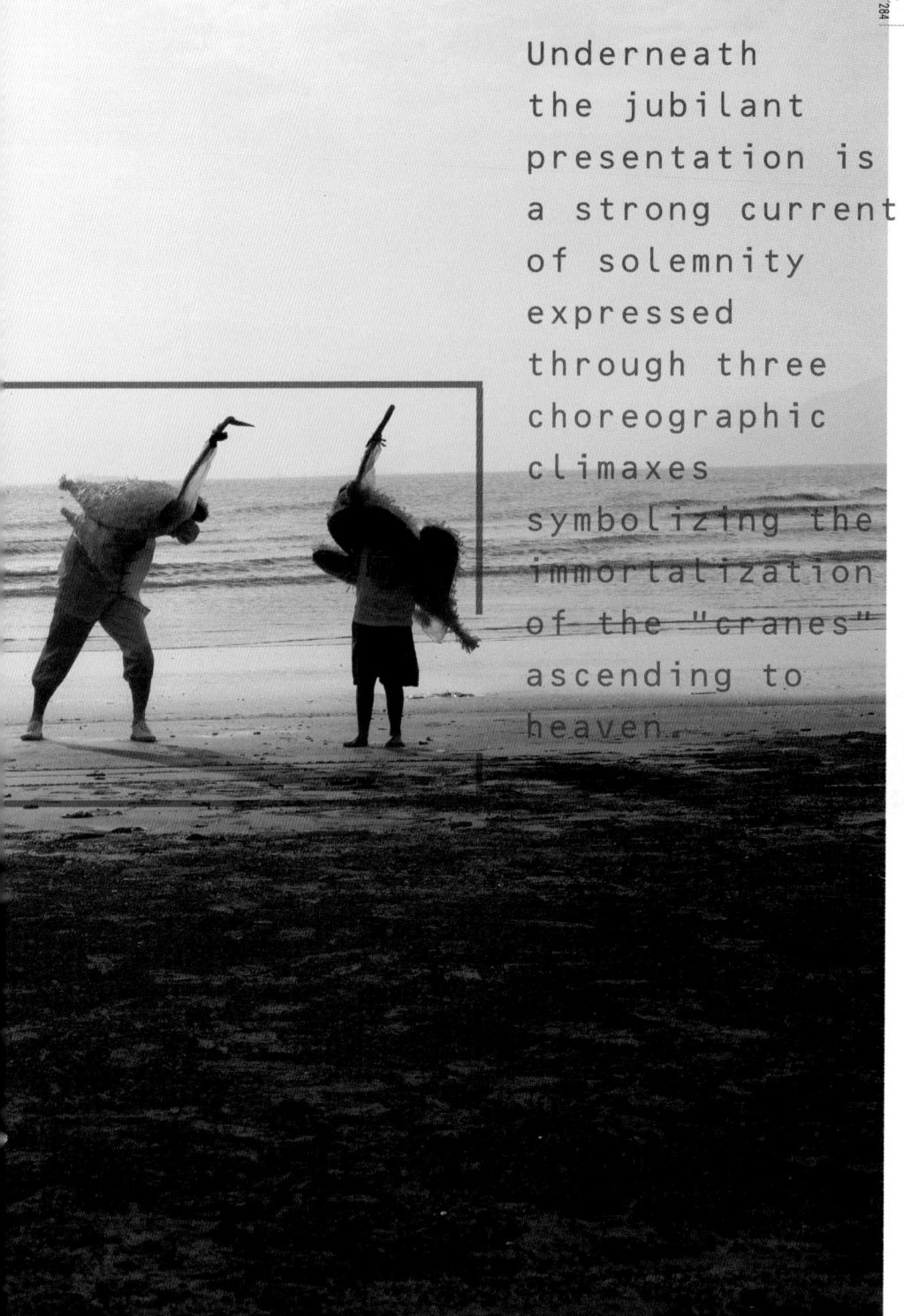

Underneath the jubilant presentation is a strong current of solemnity expressed through three choreographic climaxes symbolizing the immortalization of the "cranes" ascending to heaven.

BOAT WEDDING OF DOUMEN

The "Boat wedding" was created by the ancestors of Doumen's current residents. Located at the southwestern tip of the Pearl River Delta, Doumen is regarded as Zhuhai's cultural "treasure house". Strewn with a network of waterways characteristic of south China in ancient times, Doumen is also known as the hometown of more than 160,000 overseas Chinese. It is well-known for a dazzling collection of famed delicacies and cultural traditions, including its "boat wedding" tradition—an elaborate ceremony that includes as many as 13 rituals.

The intriguing wedding tradition spawned a group of famous "wedding planners", one of whom is Feng Beihai, whose blazing singing style is considered by the locals as "superb". One of the major figures in the inheritance of the tradition is Guo Xingfu, who makes a living as a "boat wedding singer". Interestingly, his given name "xingfu" means "happiness"—the ultimate goal of two people tying the knot.

Shatian Folk Song

A defining element in the vitality of the boat wedding tradition of Doumen is the Shatian folk song, or colloquially "xian shui ge", that has a history believed to date back to the Eastern Jin times (317-420) of China. With its sonorous vocal presentation resembling today's a cappella, this invigorating ballad form is an important source of today's "Cantopop".

chinese 飘色

fLoating coLors

As the children look around charmingly in their own innocent and enchanting way, the storybook world around them seems to come to life.

"*piao se*" in the Qing Dynasty

"*Piao se*" (literally "floating colors"), is believed to be an invention of people living in today's Guangdong Province in the late Ming Dynasty (1368-1644), with the tradition's variation in Qianwu Town considered to be an outstanding representative of this entertaining float parade incorporating all kinds of elements, including acrobatics and conjuring.

In the old times, the uproarious parade brought a ray of joy into the hard, isolated life of islanders, opening a surreal world for worn-out fishermen to restore their energy for another day's toil on the furious billows. The tradition remains an integral part in the festival scene of today's Zhuhai people.

The "floating colors" are presented by little children, normally aged 7-8, wearing flamboyant make-up and costumes designed for a specific role and the mise-en-scene, typically drawn from Chinese classical literature and folktales. Throughout the parade, the children, or the "colors", are "fastened" to a magnificently decorated platform (called "*se ban*") that is held mid-air by a group of husky men, creating an uncanny flow of dazzling colors floating in the air when viewed from a distance.

The children, called "color boys" and "color girls", are essential to the engaging charm of the parade, seeming to cast a magic spell. As the children look around charmingly in their own innocent and enchanting way, the storybook world around them seems to come to life.

佛 家 拳
fojia kung fu

OLD TALES & SECRETS

Living in Lishan Village in Qianwu Town, Zhuhai, Huang Buyun is a brilliant representative of "Fojia Kung Fu", now under city-level, cultural relics protection. The 70-year-old martial arts master is an outstanding member of the fifth generation of his "kung fu" family.

Falling into the "Nanquan" (also known as "Southern Fist") category, "Fojia Kung Fu" is believed to have been brought far afield to present-day Doumen District in Zhuhai by warrior monks of the Shaolin Temple at some point in the war-torn, late Ming Dynasty (1368-1644). Learning widely from other kung fu genres, it features a positioning technique called "monkey and horse", stressing a balance between fierce punching speed and power, and "softness" and flexibility. The swift transition between different stances and varying speeds creates a visual feast for the viewer and causes a shiver that runs down one's spine.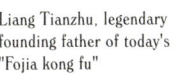

Liang Tianzhu, legendary founding father of today's "Fojia kong fu"

Zhua

OLD TALES & SECRETS

Catching Mudfish

裝 泥 魚

ng Ni Yu

In Zhuhai's Doumen area, catching sea mudfish with hand-woven, bamboo baskets has been a tradition in today's Qianwu Town for more than 240 years. In the Qianlong years of the Qing Dynasty (1644-1912), people living in the villages in the area of Qianwu Town made ends meet by catching sea mudfish on the tidal flat for trading in other places across Guangdong Province. The slippery fish served as a primary source of income for most of the residents in Hushan Village till the 1950s.

In the course of more than two centuries, villagers invented a full outfit of indigenous items, such as a special type of sliding board for gliding on the muddy shoal and "oyster socks"—something like today's waterproof rain boots. The practice, together with the bamboo basket craftsmanship, was inscribed in the national cultural heritage list in 2010.

The slippery fish served as a primary source of income for most of the residents in Hushan Village till the 1950s.

CATCHING MUDFISH

Revolutionary Road
Woodblock Print Artist, Gu Yuan

Coast Gallery
Zhuhai's New Art-and-Lifestyle Statement

WUYONG: Anti-fashion
Ma Ke's "Useless", Home-spun Charm

Back to Basics
An Dong

Joie de Vivre
A Fertile Ground for Creativity and the Artsy Life

REVOLUTIONARY
Woodblock Print Artist, Gu Yuan

古元

CHIC, KALEIDOSCOPIC, ARTSY

ROAD

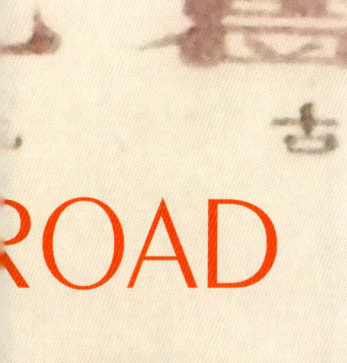

In the summer of 1938, 19-year-old Gu Yuan saluted a secretary of the Guangzhou branch of the Eighth Route Army and set off on his "revolutionary road" taking him to Yan'an, the "red heart" of the country. Diving into the struggle to win the war, the all-encompassing, anti-Japanese atmosphere in Yan'an inspired the young man, urging him to reach the limits of his creativity as an artist every day. Willing to help in any way he could, he became involved in all sorts of activities—making murals, designing wall newspapers, writing revolutionary slogans, and trying woodblock prints for the first time, never suspecting that this last specialty would become his artistic focus and passion for the rest of his life. The solid foundation laid by the daily paint-from-life practice in his younger years soon brought him into the newly-established Lu Xun Academy of Literature and Arts in Yan'an, a wartime creation of Mao Zedong that cultivated a seminal group of artists for China at a time of famine entangled with gunsmoke and mortal combat. Gu Yuan was, from the start, one of the moving forces at the school.

Due to a serious lack of painting materials in Yan'an, Gu Yuan turned to sharp knives and blocks of wood to vent his artistic passion. Scarcity, instead of being a barrier, was an impetus of creativity; and the duplicability of woodcuts also made this art form ideal for anti-Japanese publicity.

After graduation from the school, Gu Yuan threw himself into the challenging but exhilarating life of the "jiefangqu" (liberated areas). The first stop on his "art expedition" was Nianzhuang, in Chuankou, Yan'an, where living in cave dwellings with the villagers was quite an experience for the young man. Dying to practice what he had learned, Gu Yuan volunteered to be the village's culture teacher and secretary. He made printed pictures, using livestock as the running theme, for the village's anti-illiteracy campaign. The villagers quickly adapted to their new cultural life, learning to read basic characters such as "cattle", "horse" and "sheep" and loving the pictures so much that they took them home to share.

As trust and appreciation grew, communication deepened, moving Gu Yuan toward new perceptions and sensitivities, even a new, shared language of images that brought him to the first peak in his art life. More often than not, Gu Yuan got unrestrained approval from the villagers. But his art style matured and grew

离婚诉 古元 1943

Eve
dee
inc
rep
for
in
rea

Gu Yuan (1919-1996)

Born in Nazhou Village, Tangjiawan in Zhuhai. An outstanding representative of the "Yan'an-style" woodblock print art of China.

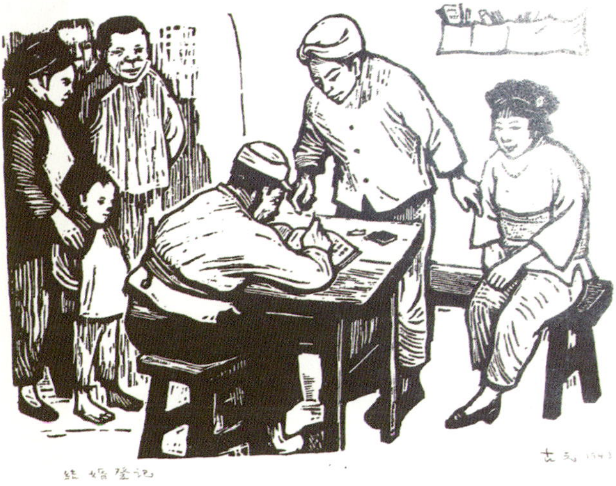

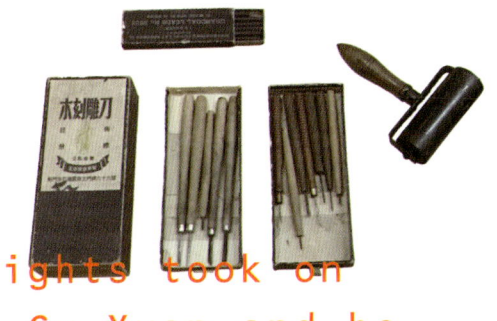

day routine sights took on
meaning for Gu Yuan and he
orated them into his unique
toire of imagery, portraying,
nstance, two farmers engaged
tting the fodder of the day

even more distinctive with the villagers' straightforward and outspoken criticism of the mistakes he made in his "farmer life" creations.

"You know, a shepherd never sets off on a day's work without taking a dog and carrying a jute bag in case of new lambs being born on the grazing site."

Everyday routine sights took on deeper meaning for Gu Yuan and he incorporated them into his unique repertoire of imagery, portraying, for instance, two farmers engaged in getting the fodder of the day ready. The act of hoeing becomes a representative action in the style of the artist's "revolutionary era", crystalizing into a charming combination of the fine and smooth Soviet woodprint aesthetics and the unvarnished paper-cutting technique used by people living in northwestern Shaanxi Province. The power of mannual workers is vividly brought out by the masculine tension bulging underneath the sleeveless shirt. In the distance, a child sits adoringly with a donkey, whose docile eyes are filled to the brim with motherly affection.

"This is the first time I saw an artwork that presents the liberated area in such a peaceful, sweet way, so much so that I feel my yearning to go there and take a look at the place that was so full of life; and it takes a lot more than skills to portray a scene through someone's back," Chinese ink painting master Xu Beihong said as he gazed into the woodcut piece for a long time at the national exhibition held in Chongqing in 1942. Xu was so impressed by the artistic flair of Gu Yuan that he bought the piece and later published an article to declare his discovery of "a rare genius in the artist circles of China".

Critics have always noted the striking uniqueness of Gu Yuan's woodcut works. "Down-to-earth" is the perfect adjective to describe the woodprint style of Gu Yuan. The cruelty of war and elemental struggle of human existence is expressed euphemistically—through the eyes and faces that contain rich emotion. The artist has always maintained a placid attitude toward social wrangling in his own life and focused instead on the everyday life of ordinary people—their little blessings and annoyances, and the way they bear them patiently as they keep working—making his creations resonate at once with historic realities and timeless beauty.

In 1941, Gu Yuan was sworn in as the director of the art workshop of Lu Xun Academy of Literature and Arts in Yan'an. The period from 1941 to 1949 saw the artist furthering his "red motif" in a diversity of styles. The decades after 1949 formed his "reminiscence period", in which he released all his homesickness in a series of refreshing landscape works represented by *The Banyan Tree* and *Fishing Girl*.

Only a couple months after Gu Yuan donated many of his artworks and personal belongings to his hometown, the artist passed away.

运草 古元 1940

Gu Yuan Museum of Art
古元美术馆

The artist's long career can be savored by people today at the Gu Yuan Museum of Art, one of the cultural hallmarks of the city of Zhuhai. Located on East Meihua Road in New Xiangzhou, it is the first city art museum in Zhuhai. The 10,000-sqm sprawl includes a whole first floor dedicated to the great artist, and serves as a key component of the country's print art training and research network. For the more exploratory type, the artist's former residence in Nazhou Village, Tangjiawan offers a glimpse into his ancestral past.

COAST GALLERY

Zhuhai's New Art-and-Lifestyle Statement

CHIC, KALEIDOSCOPIC, ARTSY

美術館
無界

With its wonderful geographical setting, Coastal Park is the ideal, welcoming gateway, creating a lively, modern-art scene and funky junction where vibrant economic development and technology can mix up with the city's maritime culture to produce a truly impressive showcase for the city's progressive, long-term development. It brings cultural and avant-garde artists together into one area, attracting strong interest, not only in Zhuhai, but from other cities and countries worldwide.

Opened in 2018 in the Gree Coast area in Tangjiawan as the city's first coastal art space, Coastal Park is a truly artsy and lively "Utopia" where "free souls" belong. Nestled along a 1.5km stretch of the city's mesmerizing coastline where the historical remnants of Tangjiawan and the energy of the ocean intermingle, it encompasses an array of delightful facilities and features Coast Gallery, Coast Bookstore and Coast Cinema, and offers a tantalizing glimpse into the city's latest art-and-lifestyle scene.

The Coast Gallery is undoubtedly the most striking building in the Coast Park sprawl. The large, futuristic space, dominated by its arch, is drenched in the purity of white, flavored by aesthetic details plucking at the long-lost innocence in the hearts of visitors and making urban numbness impossible. The smooth curves that merge the roof, floor and the walls into one unit seem to be gravity-defying and magically eliminate all boundaries. The glass windows flood the space with brilliant light. The gentle flow of air preps every visitor for entering into a brand new dimension where art and life is as indivisible as flesh and blood.

The lighting of the gallery is streamlined with the structural layout, following the visitor like a gentle halo and creating a charming feeling throughout the visitor's route among the space's various areas. The intoxicating cool-dark blends into the illumination at the gallery's souvenir shop, easing into a stream of light rays—hope from the power of art—at the end of the tunnel.

Here, people with a passion for beauty congregate to break boundaries and indulge in expressive freedom, to present the originality and charm of modern art in a way that cannot be experienced in other art spaces. Striving to embrace the spirit of "no boundaries", the gallery is open to all artists attempting to express their message in and about this changing world, regardless of social status and backgrounds. The works in the collection of the gallery are not in imitation of Western art or repetitions of traditional works. Instead they seek to overcome the existing framework of art. Exhibitions are rich in depth and quality, and wide in scope. It is an interactive gallery—a place of meeting, understanding each other and creating together.

COAST GALLERY

WUYONG 無用
ANTI-FASHION

Ma Ke's "Useless", Home-spun Charm

CHIC KALEIDOSCOPIC ARTSY

Ma Ke graduated from the Suzhou Institute of Silk Textile Technology in 1992, and subsequently studied women's wear at Central Saint Martins. In 1996, she established her first clothing label, EXCEPTION de Mixmind, currently sold in the label's own shops in China, with major retail presence in Shanghai, Beijing and Guangzhou. Their collections are comprised of women's clothing made from locally sourced cotton, silk, linen and wool, and include other accessories and items.

Ma Ke is among the youngest of the first generation of Chinese fashion designers who have received international acclaim, and she is the first Chinese to show at Paris Haute Couture, with her subtle, organic and reflective clothing, creative and experimental in shape and classically oriental in style. Ma Ke is best known abroad for her two WUYONG collections: WUYONG/the Earth, which debuted at Paris Fashion Week Spring Summer 2007; and WUYONG/Qing Pin, which was held on July 3, 2008 as her first show for Paris Haute Couture.

Confronted by a local clothing industry with cheap, homogenizing mass-production and poorly paid workers whose skills were assigned no value, and by a fashion scene lacking local aesthetic influence, dominated by foreign labels, she dedicated herself to developing her "useless" ideas; that is, to breathe new life into time-honored professions and traditions that, otherwise, could well have faded to grey in a generation or two.

"I left my comfort zone to find a new direction by traveling to remote villages, where I realized what I could do and wanted to do," Ma Ke explained in tracing her eureka moment. The result was a breakup with her first clothing label, EXCEPTION, and the birth of "WUYONG", literally meaning "useless".

Her rise to international fame is largely because of her use of environmentally friendly fabrics and recycled materials, and for their manufacture using traditional dyeing, weaving and embroidery techniques, most notably those of the Dong people of Southern

Ma Ke

A Chinese fashion designer and founder of two clothing labels: EXCEPTION de Mixmind, a ready-to-wear line started in 1996; and WUYONG, an haute couture line founded in 2006 and based in Zhuhai. In 2005, she presented her clothing at the Shenzhen Biennale of Urbanism and Architecture; and in 2008, her fashion house WUYONG was appointed as a Guest Member of the Chambre Syndicale de la Haute Couture in France. In 2009, her work found its way into the National Art Museum of China.

China. Despite her soft nature, her unorthodox shows and anti-consumerist statements have earned Ma Ke a reputation for being anti-fashion. However, she is equally lauded for her conscientious efforts to preserve traditions and protect the environment. It must have taken a steely sense of determination and iron-cast belief in herself to build what now is essentially her WUYONG empire.

Ma Ke's first two shows for WUYONG, held more than a year apart, were distinctive for their absence of runways and for incorporating certain elements of performance art. In 2007, Ma Ke was invited to present her first collection, titled WUYONG/the Earth, at Paris Fashion Week. The show was held in the gymnasium of the Lycée Stanislas. Rather than presenting the collection on a catwalk as in a traditional fashion show, Ma Ke had the models stand motionless on tall, illuminated plinths arranged on the gymnasium floor. The audience was invited to walk amongst the models and examine the clothing up-close. The show was a triumph: Elle magazine called Ma Ke's Paris debut "brilliant... one of the great moments of the season." The collection was later put on display at the gallery Joyce Palais-Royal from March 1 to April 6, 2007.

In 2008, Ma Ke was invited to reprise WUYONG/the Earth as part of the Fashion in Motion (live catwalk) events held at the Victoria & Albert Museum in London. Three performances were given in the Raphael Gallery on May 16, 2008. Concurrently, a piece from the collection was on display in the museum's China Design Now exhibition.

Ma Ke's far-flung studio/factory, set in a weather-beaten garden in Tangjia where the city's urban sprawl gives way to historic remnants and ruins, is a world within itself, dripping with creativity, grace and oriental beauty. It produces the WUYONG collections, employing a team of workers skilled in traditional clothing manufacturing techniques. All stages of production are done in-house, including the spinning, weaving, dyeing and sewing; even using traditional equipment such

The studio is an extension of Ma Ke's personality: dreamy, bursting with ideas, sprawling.

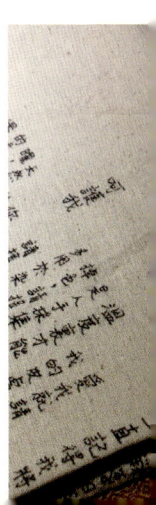

WUYONG/Qing Pin, held on July 3, 2008 as Ma Ke's first show for Paris Haute Couture.

as a Chinese loom dating from the 19th century. Some of the articles in the collections either incorporate or are fashioned out of recycled material and found objects, including a paint-covered sheet made into a dress and an old tarpaulin constructed into an over-sized coat.

This living, breathing fashion house in Tangjia represents the delicate, artistic vision of its softly spoken creator, who loves to collect traditional Chinese trinkets, ornaments and eye-catching curios. Here is a woman with vision and, crucially, the fearlessness

to see her vision through. The studio is an extension of Ma Ke's personality: dreamy, bursting with ideas, sprawling.

The designer launched her Beijing "Wu Yong" station in Beijing in 2014. A remake of a former factory site behind the CAFA Art Museum, it marked a new start in Ma Ke's rebuilding of her fashion philosophy.

"People push the door open and walk into the space, their eyes welling up because of the long-lost feeling of coming back to the basics—the roots."

In 2007, Ma Ke starred in the award-winning documentary *Useless* by Chinese director Jia Zhangke. Depicting the Chinese garment industry, the documentary recorded her Paris Fashion Week sensation. The film won the Orizzonti Doc Prize at the 64th Venice Film Festival in 2007. Ma Ke also designed costumes for singer Dadawa's concert *Singing in Heaven* (2001).

BACK TO BASICS
An Doong

CHIC, KALEIDOSCOPIC, ARTSY

AN DONG: BACK TO BASICS

An Dong
Oil artist and Director of the Exhibition Department of Zhuhai Museum; an outstanding representative of the China's "Shu Xiang" Art Movement in its later stage.

In April 2007, 120 artworks by Zhuhai-based artist, An Dong, were presented at the Fukuoka Art Museum in Ohori-Koen Park, blessed with beautiful waters and greenery, and left visitors holding their breath in deep concentration—and awe. With a proud collection including works of artists representing 20th century art, such as Miro, Dali, Chagall, Warhol, Delvaux and Brancusi as well as Japanese masters of modern Western-style painting, it took the museum three years of observation to send the invitation letter to An Dong. The artworks of An Dong encapsulate the quintessence of Chinese characters and reject the constricting fences of the "Orient" context, pointing directly at the dream-like, yet overwhelming essence of modern art, the museum representatives commented.

Born in Xinjiang Uygur Autonomous Region, An Dong felt directionless after graduation from Guangxi Arts University. He uprooted himself by moving from the dry heat of the northwest to settle down on the balmy coasts of Zhuhai, a city he calls "open enough for me to communicate freely with the world" and "quiet enough for me to concentrate on my whimsy".

An Dong describes his Zhuhai years as the start of steering his artistic gaze from his "red, wild northwest character" to his "blue abstractionism". On the breezy coasts, the man's soul was set free. He finally found his own "language" and has been holding fast to it ever since; and the city's artsy milieu makes him relaxed and always inspired.

1999 was a defining, "epiphany" year for An Dong. During a trip to France that he recalls as "a spiritual typhoon that swept his soul", his inner tangle suddenly defused into revelation about the elusive charm and modernity of "abstractionism". The

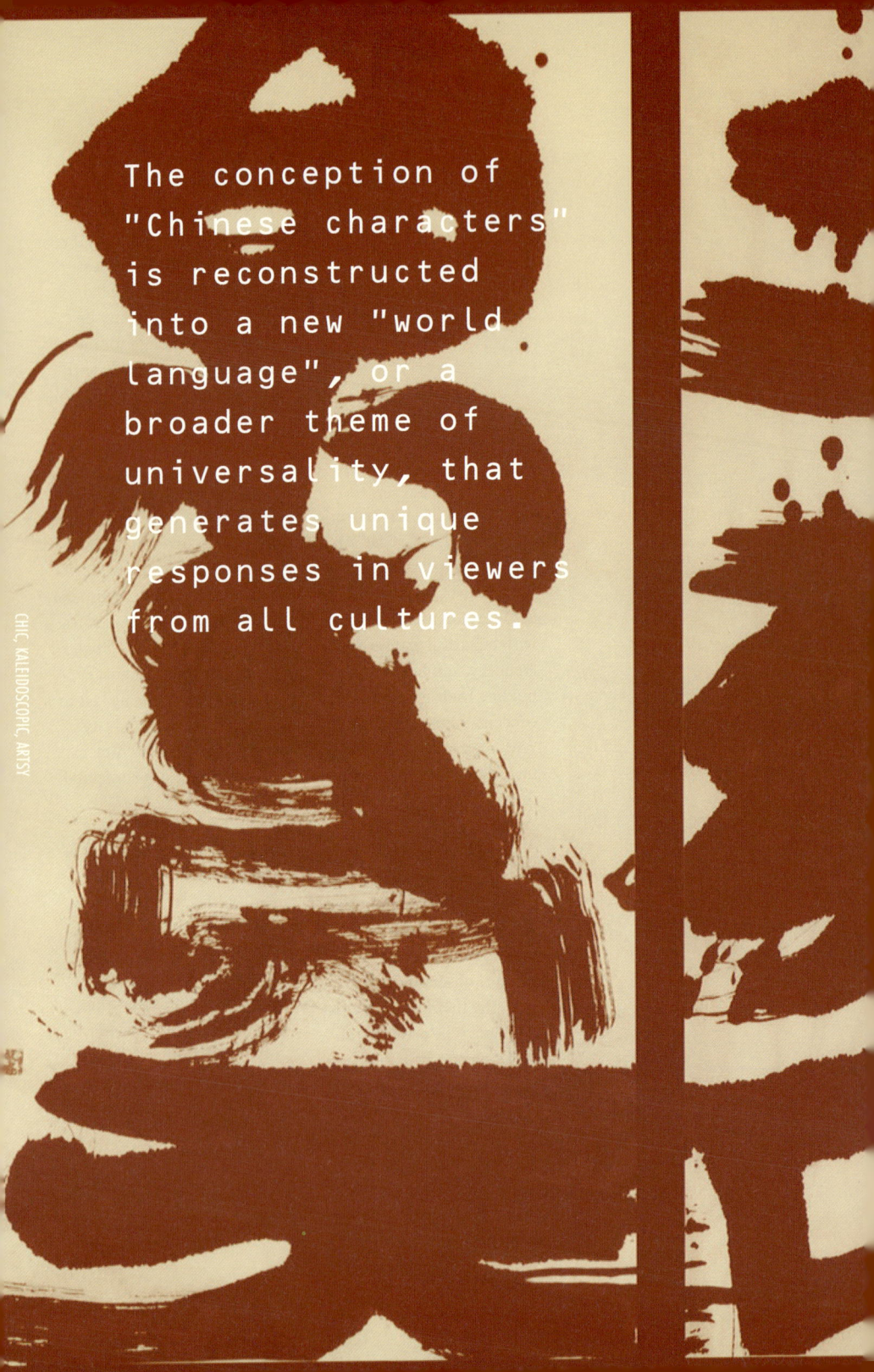

The conception of "Chinese characters" is reconstructed into a new "world language", or a broader theme of universality, that generates unique responses in viewers from all cultures.

"Shu Xiang"
书／象

An avant-garde art movement originating in China of the 1980s. The earlier representatives of the art movement include Qiu Zhenzhong, Xu Bing and Gu Wenda.

realization came like a fresh wind, putting the spring back in his step. Back in Zhuhai, he switched his artistic focus from oil creation to ink and calligraphy, pursuing the "truth" of art for the next 15 years.

Starting 1999, the artistic gaze of An Dong turned to "Shu Xiang"**, an avant-garde art movement originated in the 1980s in China. "Shu Xiang" strives to rediscover the beauty of Chinese characters and explores the infinite artistic possibilities hidden in an ancient pictographic writing system. Through the thick, fierce brushstrokes that passionately soar across the canvas, the viewer is taken vicariously on an emotional journey. The brilliance of Chinese culture is woven into new contexts that direct the viewer into the future.

Through "Shu Xiang", An Dong prompts the viewer to reassess Chinese characters as well as the culture in a different light. In his creations under the theme that appears more calligraphic than the art of painting in the traditional sense, the enchanting soul of the characters emerges through painfully minimalistic contours that contain immense depths. The unrestrained markings play on the imagination of the viewer, providing clues but also space for one's thoughts to run wild. The conception of "Chinese characters" is reconstructed into a new "world language", or a broader theme of universality, that generates unique responses in viewers from all cultures.

The Future

Taken from the Past

Beishan Neighborhood / But More Than Books / West Side Story

JOIE DE VIVRE

A Fertile Ground for Creativity and the Artsy Life

CHIC, KALEIDOSCOPIC, ARTSY

Creative

May
Beishan World Music Festival

October
Beishan International Jazz Festival

Tingyun Bookstore

Bei Shan Ju

Xiaomi Bakery

Suhe Vegetarian Lifestyle

CREATIVE BEISHAN

北山 Beishan

An Amazing Concentration of Emerging Variations on Ancient Themes

*Th*e charm of the city's Beishan neighborhood—the cultural, if not geographical, heart of Zhuhai—is its juxtaposition of old and new, and a stunning blend of art and life. Here, tradition is not ossified, but feted along with innovation and joie de vivre. Everything here is profoundly artsy, yet somehow homey and natural at the same time. Indulge in the village's electrifying music seasons or revel in the peace and quiet of this urban sanctuary; it all depends on your moods. Temples, ancestral halls and Republican theaters coexist with so-chic-it-hurts art galleries, stylish breakfast-and-bed places, snazzy restaurants, al fresco spots, exquisite florists and heartfelt bakeries; jazz schools and "guqin" studios stand in harmony with Mahjong parlors, dumpling vendors and wet markets, complete with avant-garde sculptures and a limitless, twinkling flow of Chopin's "Impromptu" interlacing with the fragrance of jazz.

Get lost in the Bright Light City's Music Madness

It's good for a city to have its own music festival. It's great to have more than one!

GET LOST IN THE BRIGHT LIGHTS OF THE CITY'S MUSIC MADNESS

Beishan woke up from its 300-year slumber with the soulful melody of jazz streaming into the starry sky one magical night eight years ago. Now hosting two heavyweight music festivals that draw participation that is truly international, including the universally-loved, three-time Grammy winner Ricardo Vogt and his new band Vogt4Us, in the 2018 event. This historic village is a mind-blowing introduction to the urban charm and music madness of modern Zhuhai.

The quiet neighborhood was lit up again on the night of May 4 in 2018, with the passion of screaming fans beamed into the homes of people all over Zhuhai. Closing with the eclectic glory of World Music from Saharadja (Indonesia's top world music band), two days were soaked in a palette of international rhythms that broke down global barriers and emanated love and peace.

The 2018 Beishan World Music Festival brought in eight world-renowned bands from seven countries/regions that took everyone on a journey through the melodies of nations from around the world. The event saw the debut of SISAY, whose sincere, profound music, rooted in the mountains and rivers of Ecuador, is a perfect match with the "Renaissance" of Beishan. An old friend of the music festival, Ricardo Vogt grabbed the audience's ears again with his magic guitar developed exclusively to utilize a string that produces a very characteristic and original sound.

The two-day revelry also included a plethora of related activities that used music as the "Esperanto" to inspire education, community redevelopment, architecture conservation and other art practices such as photography and painting. For music fans who missed out on the May carnival, the annual Zhuhai Jazz Music Festival is only five months away. The 2017 jazz party feasted the ears of the audience with a program glorified by six bands and Canadian pianist David Braid, considered one of his country's most celebrated jazz players and a true "Renaissance man" when it comes to music.

2018 BEISHAN WO

The festival's "Resident Musicians" program, designed to encourage exposure of local folk music on a global stage, turned out a sensational success. In fact, the charming placement of Zhuhai's indigenous music with the accompaniment of piano and bass marks the coming of age of Beishan Music Festival as the magnetic music brand it now is. With the seeds of music sown in the soil of Beishan, the brand has gone beyond the musical facade of one place and genre to reach deeper cultural connections, evolving symbiotically with this ancient, lively neighborhood.

BEISHAN JAZZ FESTIVAL 2017

EYOT (SERBIA)

UNIVERSAL SKY FEAT. DAMIEN PRUD'HOMME (FRANCE, GERMANY)

HANG EM HIGH (SWITZERLAND, AUSTRIA, POLAND)

CANNONBAL (AUSTRALIA)

BORN TO BE BLUE QUARTET (CANADA)

2017 BiJF Line-up

EYOT (Serbia)
The proud representative of a new generation of European musicians, this Serbian quartet breaks all temporal, geographical and cultural boundaries of Balkan Jazz, explosively blending classical music, art-rock and traditional melodies.

Universal Sky feat. Damien Prud' homme (France, Germany)
A project that is all about eliminating boundaries and using music to share emotions.

Hang Em High (Switzerland, Austria, Poland)
Hot like melted iron, cool as Clint Eastwood.

Cannonbal (Australia)
Inspired by the jazz/groove/soul music of the late saxophone giant Julian "Cannonball" Adderley. Heavy Blues and gospel influence combined with a deep, infectious groove.

Born To Be Blue Quartet (Canada)
Described by *The New York Observer* as "authentic and sophisticated".

Mathias Heise Quadrillion (Denmark)
One of very few jazz harmonica players in Denmark, and very much inspired by the fusion genre.

MATHIAS HEISE QUADRILLION (DENMARK)

CHIC, KALEIDOSCOPIC, ARTSY

BEISHAN WORLD MUSIC FESTIVAL

(2018) Vogt4Us (Brazil / Australia)
Three-time Grammy Award winner

(2017) Celtic Social Club (France)
It gave its first concert in front of 50,000 spectators.

(2016) Bogus (Belgium)
The trio has been playing together since the age of 13.

(2015) Juan Pollo Raffo Quatet (Argentina)
Pollo has led various influential groups in the Argentinean contemporary popular music scene.

(2012) Funf (Hong Kong)
"Funf came on and tore the house down."

(2013) Youn Sun Nah and Ulf Wakenius (Korea / Sweden)
The voice of Korea jazz.

(2011) Chop Suey Milkshake (Hong Kong / Nepal)
This eclectic group of four uses a mix of melodic and percussive sounds to create a Blues-like music that exhibits all the shades of the participating instruments.

(2014) Ray Lema VSNP Quintet (France)
Ray Lema's skills as a pianist are said to be unsurpassable.

BEISHAN WORLD MUSIC FESTIVAL 2018

The "revolution" of Beishan all started in the artistic gaze of Xue Yihan, the artist father of Simone Xue and his brother Xue Jun.

The Renaissance of An Urban Village

THE RENAISSANCE OF AN URBAN VILLAGE

Wrapped within the artsy façade and musical pulse of present-day Beishan is a man's reverence for tradition and passion for architectural heritage. In a sense, the village's musical pride is far overshadowed by its key significance in China's "village revitalization" movement.

The "revolution" of Beishan all started in the artistic gaze of Xue Yihan, the artist father of Simone Xue and his brother Xue Jun. The two masterminded not only the striking neighborhood but also the unique musical milieu of Beishan. Before a fatal heart attack in 2008, the woodblock print artist spent an abundance of time admiring the hundred-year-old architecture and talking the villagers into a salvage project that was to start with the restoration of ancestral temples. The relay baton was subsequently taken by his two sons, both crazy about art and staunchly refusing to kowtow to the march of reckless gentrification.

In 2008, restoration of a set of four of the village's signature buildings started. The result was an art studio and art gallery set in the original structure of ancient temple buildings, and a new Beishan Theater converted from a dilapidated village theater first built in the Republican times of China.

For the first couple years, Simone was not sure exactly what to do with the theater, but inspiration struck one day when he was chatting with his music-loving French friend Jean-Jacques Verdun. Over a few cups of coffee, the blueprint of what has evolved into the best music festival brand in southern China was drawn, although the devoted son could never have predicted that he would see the village grow with such a potent glory—far more than enough to reward all the struggles his father endured.

The winding lanes are still the same ones the forefathers of today's villagers, living in their brick-wood houses, walked for hundreds of years.

Jazz and the melodic strains of piano made the urban village once again a focal point of the community and a bewitching place where East meets West. However, the winding lanes are still the same ones the forefathers of today's villagers, living in their brick-wood houses, walked for hundreds of years. Throughout the restoration, the village's original social fabric, together with cultural essentials and the local lifestyle, has been perfectly retained. The rebirth of Beishan has produced something that those many overdone "ancient villages" gone Disney cannot even approximate. The Xue brothers are driven by a painful awareness of how fragile yet crucial this local "sense of place" can be. It is just such a mentality and broad vision that makes Beishan much more than a simple collection of trendy international entertainments and, rather, a series of unique experiences involving the precious chemistry between tradition and creative experimentation.

The "invisible" entrance of Bei Shan Ju reflects the place's "un-designed" charm.

THE RENAISSANCE OF AN URBAN VILLAGE

Zhuhai's Joie de Vivre

It is a sanctuary for people to get together in, hang out, listen to music, dress up and express themselves.

During intervals in the village's music seasons, the former Beishan Theater, now named Goodone, serves as a showroom and "Warehouse of Old Things", featuring "retro bricks" (originals left over from reconstruction) in a variety of colors, on display and for sale. Walking through the rusty iron gate of the theater, one's eyes first land on the stunning example of Victorian-style brickwork, with attention next being drawn to a wonderfully diverse range of vintage items that fashion junkies will find it hard to keep their hands off, from classic clothing, adorable clutch bags and locally designed jewelry to brick-shaped chocolates, postcards and writing cases.

Very cool stuff fills every corner of this intriguing space. However, the "warehouse" is more than just a chance to buy unique gifts; it is a sanctuary for people to get together in, hang out, listen to music, dress up and express themselves. It acts as a kind of headquarters for the city's fashionable and creative minds. This power to bring people together makes the "warehouse" the beloved venue in the city's pop culture scene that it is.

Many of the products here are the brainchild of the "warehouse staff", nicknamed "brick workwomen", their most recent creation being a collection of garments made from fabrics woven on old-fashioned looms that were once used by a local textile mill in the 1960s.

Raymond Loewy, whose daring genius revolutionized industrial design, lived by his own famous "MAYA principle"—Most Advanced Yet Acceptable: "The adult public's taste is not necessarily ready to accept the logical solutions to their requirements if the solution implies too vast a departure from what they have been conditioned into accepting as the norm."

Bei Shan Ju, remolded from two dorm buildings previously housing migrant workers in the urban village, serves as a beautiful, if accidental, example of the magic of MAYA.

CHIC KALEIDOSCOPIC ARTSY

Bei Shan Ju: Most Advanced Yet Acceptable

Opened in 2016 as the first "design hotel" in Zhuhai, Bei Shan Ju did not shoot to its fame in the fiercely competitive B&B (Bed-and-Breakfast) industry of China for no reason. It appeared as an alien, pitting itself against the massive, imitative projects that level the "old" and, in their place, erect giant clichés to accommodate the hotel and restaurant customer population.

Bei Shan Ju, now one of the essential B&Bs and points of interest for any leisurely traveler in Zhuhai, appears simple and plain, so much so that it blends beautifully into the surroundings and aplomb of the villagers who carry on, wholeheartedly as usual, in the life of the street. The design of Bei Shan Ju is "non-design" with its seemingly humble façade and non-descript entrance, yet with an indulgent use of glass that perfectly reflects the sublime but everyday images of village life. Evidently, the designer played a successful game of visual redirection by moving the gaze of passers-by towards "nothingness".

Inside, the cool greyness of thick cement walls takes over, enticing the guest into a world of fine arts, music and coffee. Illuminated with a pendant lamp from Florence, the elegant, but demure public space of Bei Shan Ju is second to none in Zhuhai, and the names of the 20 guestrooms, such as "Jazz" and "Blues", reveal the designer's fascination with classic genres. The restaurant and coffee lounge, both on the second floor, have lighting and well-considered decorative details that reinforce the atmosphere, building a wonderfully reclusive space for whiling away many musical hours.

The subtle beauty of art and timeless, comforting pace of the urban haven merges into a charming approachability. With silhouettes of passing locals, totally ignoring the existence of the building, and the four seasons rolling by, it feels like Bei Shan Ju has been there forever, like a tree grown from the Beishan soil. Its daily encounter with the villagers is, essentially, the core of this boutique lodging establishment and the embodiment of the artsy soul of the city.

> *Evidently, the designer played a successful game of visual redirection moving the gaze of passers-by toward "nothingness".*

Inside, the cool greyness of thick cement walls takes over, enticing the guest into a world of fine arts, music and coffee. Illuminated with a pendant lamp from Florence, the elegant, but demure public space of Bei Shan Ju is second to none in Zhuhai, and the names of the 20 guestrooms, such as "Jazz" and "Blues", reveal the designer's fascination with classic genres. The restaurant and coffee lounge, both on the second floor, have lighting and well-considered decorative details that reinforce the atmosphere, building a wonderfully reclusive space for whiling away many musical hours.

Sebastien Durand, a Frenchman in Zhuhai

Giraffe at Large

CHIC, KALEIDOSCOPIC, ARTSY

In Beishan, if you look up into the sky, you'll find a giraffe cocking its head to make eye contact with you. And a winking giraffe at large sure beats one in some sad enclosure.

Today's Beishan neighborhood is the perfect place to marvel at the latest and trendiest Zhuhai street fashion. It is here that the city's playful chameleon character and its heart of a child is brought into full play.

The bustling streets and the village environs are also home to many of the city's hottest venues, serving as the HQ of the animated bakery brand—Xiaomi Bakery, a popular modern music school specializing in the education and promotion of jazz culture, the Beishan Estate that hosts a refined "guqin" studio, and a chic Beijing-based vegetarian eatery where one can enjoy the high art of Chinese vegetarianism and rethink what to eat and why—if not from an ethical perspective, then a healthy one.

Xiaomi Bakery moved its HQ from the city's Oxford Street to Beishan a couple of years ago, and Sebastien Durand is seen there every day absorbed in the act of blending his fascination with Bruce Lee's Wing Chun and the principles of Daoism into truly organic and genuinely French baguettes (with a Chinese philosophical connection). Another absolute must-try in your Beishan promenade is "Buddhist Punk" Vegetarian Bistro, also a creation by Sebastien.

Rumor has it that the bakery site was originally a pig pen, giving an air of mystery as

Rumor has it that the previous life of the Xiaomi Bakery site was a sweet home of oinking piglets.

to how the place evolved into what it is today. For Sebastien, this story only adds depth and irony to his Beishan (and Zhuhai) experience.

If your preference is to return to authentic Chinese culture, the ideal place to visit is Beishan Estate, first built in 1859. The premises now houses a number of outlets selling products that represent Zhuhai's indigenous spirit, such as the traditional "*qipao*" (aka "cheongsam", in Cantonese) and a wide variety of textile crafts. The complex is a treasure box of Chinese art, design and culture that amounts to a celebration of the finer things in life, whether that be good food, refined music or an old-fashioned book that you just can't put down.

The ethereal sound of "*guqin*" only adds to the tranquility of this urban sanctuary. The time-honored, elite courtyard house was the source of enlightenment for Zhiling, who quit a fat salary from a listed company and the gaudy nightlife of the big city to settle down in this soothing hideaway, after falling for Tai Ji Quan (aka T'ai Chi) and getting incurably addicted to the angelic sound of the ancient musical instrument. Her Qinyin Tonglu "*guqin*" studio, now an iconic part of the courtyard estate and serving more than 300 students, has become the city's "*guqin*" cultural base. For Zhiling, however, the best contribution of her life in this serene settlement is seen in the studio's cultural gatherings, in which participants enjoy the cultivation and solace brought by everything that is profoundly Chinese.

In Zhuhai, you don't need a zoo to find a giraffe. There is one in Beishan, more specifically, looming above a western restaurant.

CHIC, KALEIDOSCOPIC, ARTSY

A winking giraffe at large

sure beats one in some sad enclosure.

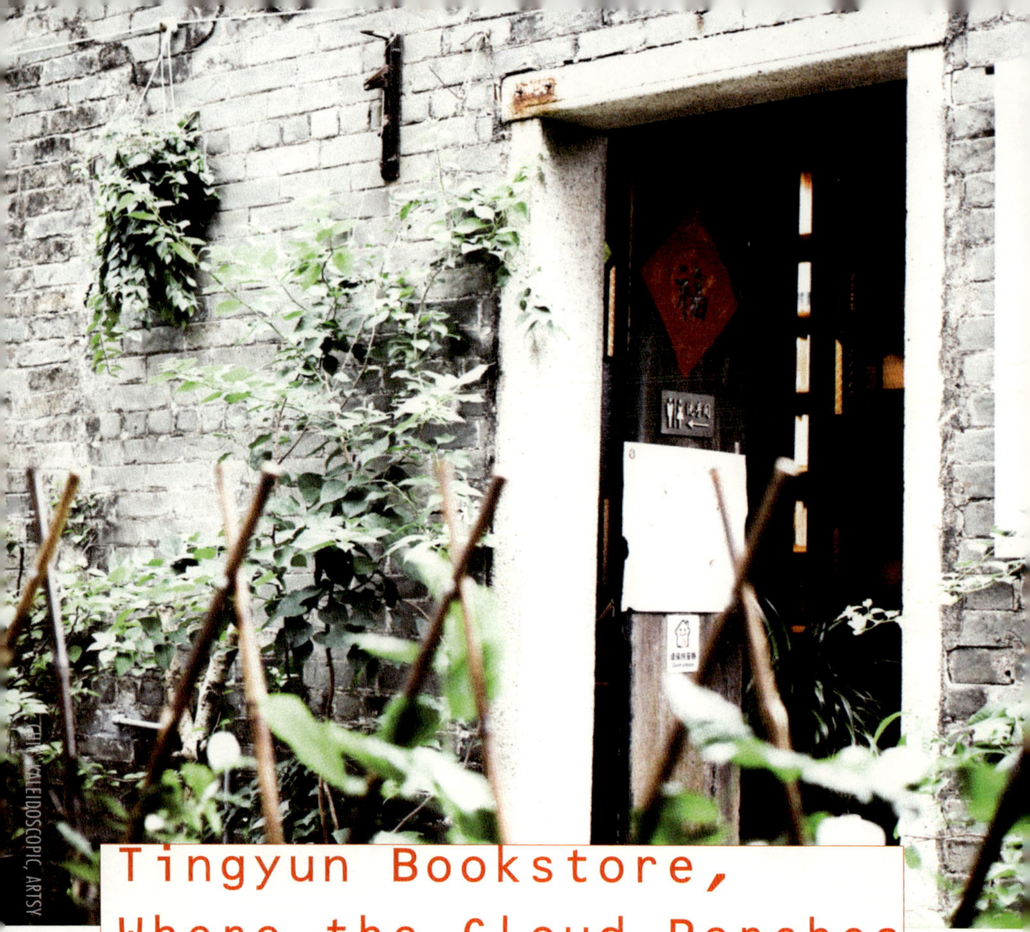

Tingyun Bookstore, Where the Cloud Perches

"I have always imagined that Paradise will be a kind of library."

— Jorge Luis Borges

TINGYUN BOOKSTORE, WHERE THE CLOUD PERCHES

Already a renowned cultural powerhouse in its own right, Tingyun Bookstore is a calm at the heart of the bustling village of Beishan, adding yet another feather to the city's artsy hat in the shape of Beishan's first ever elite book outlet, or "library", as the owner may prefer to call it. The bookstore is renowned for not only its highly selective book collection, but its creative environs, including a range of designer goods and exquisite lifestyle items.

a literary salon in which people can strengthen their cultural resolve. Indeed, the brand goes to great lengths to promote the pursuit of reading to all comers, and to make reading a part of everyday life. Tucked away next to the coffee-scented public reading space is the "secret garden" of the owner and her beloved feline friend.

This exquisite bookstore, a remake of a hundred-year-old ancestral temple site, is the brainchild of Yunduo ("Cloud"), who evidently has an ethereal, protective being around her, inspiring and guiding her efforts. The first part of the bookstore's lofty name is drawn from a poem by Southern Song poet, Xin Qiji (1140-1207). The second part of the name is pronounced, "*shufang*", which literarily means "the study" and echoes her dream of having a place for reading and contemplation where souls can be set free, and everyone can see the library of Borges around them in this Heaven on Earth.

Here, literature and art lovers of all age gather to connect with the wider cultural world, to sample the country's intellectual spirit and energy in full swing, to spend quality time with like-minded individuals, or to just browse the store's astounding selection of titles in comfort. With a coffee bar and cozy seating areas for people to gather and, perhaps, indulge in the joy of slowly reading a good, old-fashioned book, the "library" is the dream of its beautiful owner come to life: to build

CHIC, KALEIDOSCOPIC, ARTSY

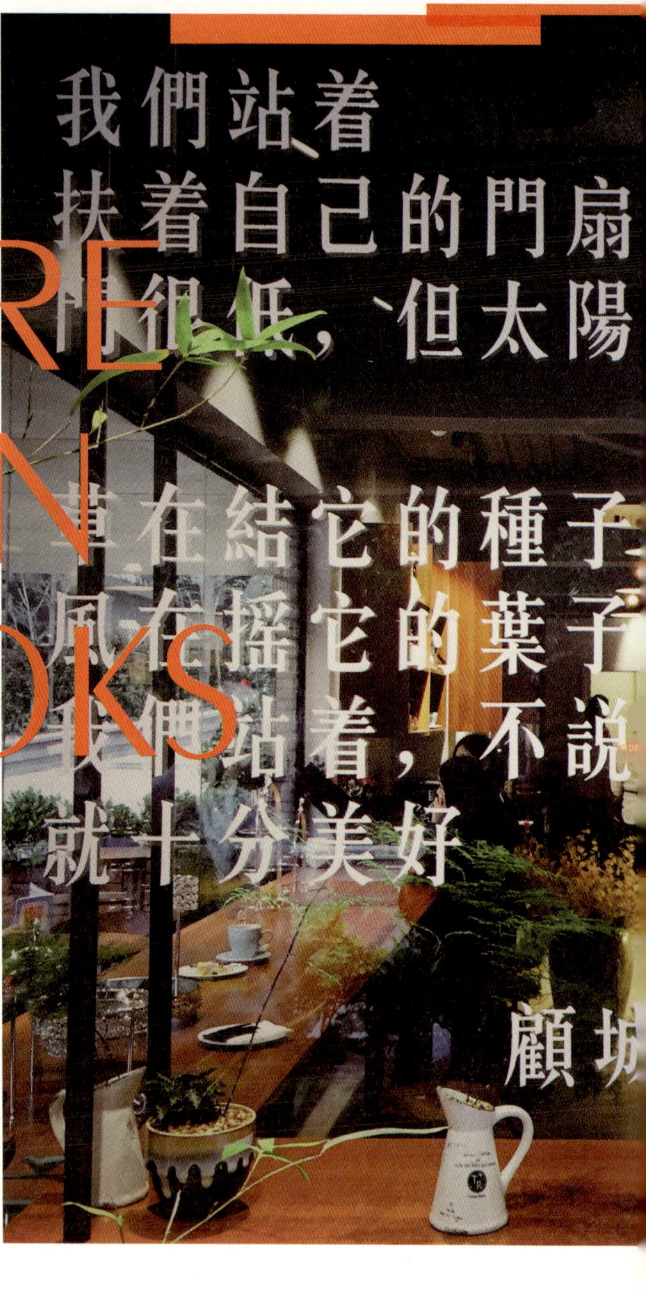

BUT MORE THAN BOOKS

我們站着
扶着自己的門扇
很低，但太陽

草在結它的種子
風在搖它的葉子
我們站着，不說
就十分美好

顧城

READZONE / Wenhua Bookstore / Coast Bookstore / Shu Sheng Guan

As most avid readers will tell you, encountering a good book can be one of the most rewarding experiences known to man.

Zhuhai is justifiably a "reading city", strewn with countless serene hideaways for book lovers. Wherever you turn, a bookstore is just around the corner. The city's unique bookstore ecology eclipses many other cities in China that are already renowned cultural powerhouses in their own right.

It is one thing to fantasize about owning a bookstore that has a jumble of rooms encouraging browsers to meander all day long; for most people, it is another thing entirely to put these romantic thoughts into action. For dreamers in Zhuhai, however, the difference is not too much to handle; and it seems that this city has somehow been spared the widespread damage done to "brick-and-mortar" bookstores elsewhere by the outbreak of electronic books and online bookstores. Bookstores are one of the most prized possessions of Zhuhai - the Muse of the city; and the joy of reading is a tangible part of everyday life here.

In 2017, Amazon China ranked Zhuhai fourth among those cities that "most love reading". The city's dizzying collection of fine bookstores sells more than books: it spreads the message that books and reading can bind lives as surely as any shared love, and adds a cultural quality to the social fabric of Zhuhai, where "no man is an island; every book is a world".

CHIC, KALEIDOSCOPIC, ARTSY

READZONE
A Cultural Happening

閱
潮

READZONE / A CULTURAL HAPPENING

Looking for a place to cool down in the scorching summer heat of southern China? In Zhuhai, you don't have to travel far and, if you prefer, always have a handy alternative to those sunny bathing beaches. The peace and the aroma of coffee at a bookstore just across the street is a perfect antidote to the fierce sun. In fact, such a pleasant oasis of shade is to be found almost anywhere in Zhuhai.

In a real sense, bookstores bring people together in this "melting pot"—they serve as a nurturing hub for print-hungry individuals in this "immigrant city" and those many who come in as strangers and walk out as friends with something in common.

The opening of Wenhua Bookstore, under the label of "Xinhua", in the boisterous neighborhood of Gongbei in 1993, had enormous cultural implications for the city. At a time when private bookstores were a rarity, Zhuhai took the lead in fostering a market-oriented ecosystem for bookstores to thrive.

The launch of the READZONE flagship location, owned by Huafa Group, in 2014, was a cultural happening for the city, and added significantly to the city's "artsy" repertoire in the shape of the first book-cum-lifestyle chain outlet to grace Zhuhai. The bookstore presents not only a comprehensive selection of categorized books and periodicals shelved together, but lures one into a stimulating environment loaded with a whole range of lifestyle items and exquisite goods of a cultural nature.

Since 2014, READZONE has expanded to include a dozen locations across Zhuhai. For book lovers in Zhuhai, READZONE has become the city's de facto cultural rendezvous point, where the city's intellectual spirit and energy can be sampled in full swing. It has also risen over the years to become a major influence in the city's art world, thanks to its regular exhibitions, wonderful art spaces and a fertile relationship with cultural elites all over the country, all the time serving as a center for people to exchange ideas and deepen their devotion to culture. Indeed, the brand goes to great lengths to promote reading for people of all ages and walks of life by providing an attractive and stimulating learning environment. With such a strong, far-reaching cultural pedigree, the opening of every new READZONE location causes a stir in the city.

In a real sense, bookstores bring people together in this "melting pot"—they serve as a nurturing hub for print-hungry individuals in this "immigrant city" and those many who come in as strangers and walk out as friends with something in common.

Bands of sunlight filter through the foliage of trees and flood in through the gigantic oval canopy of the city's chicest mall, home to the city's greatest "reading salon". Covering an area of some 1,798 square meters, the crown jewel in Zhuhai's "Cave of Wonders" ranks among the best in China's growing legions of first-tier bookstores.

This impressive flagship store is the brainchild of eminent Hong Kong designer, Kenneth Ko. As soon as you set foot into this expansive world of books, you feel elevated to a plateau of modern elegance and free-spirited simplicity as the main hallway tapers down to create a serene and solemn space for one to get into the right mood for reading. The store's charming "Literature" section is a decidedly peaceful space (even when teeming with avid readers, including whole families), innovatively laid out with stylish, cozy nooks that encourage you to unwind and lose yourself in literature.

Surrounded by the fragrance of tea and coffee, the welcoming, unpretentious atmosphere and attractively illuminated shelves lure both young and old to dive into a book, all gathering obliviously to spend quality time here by browsing the store's astounding selection of titles in comfort. Every customer's needs and wishes are attended to by the all-knowing store assistants, who silently buzz around the place assuring a problem-free environment. Every cup of coffee is crafted by master baristas from Taiwan, whose magic skills make sure everyone walks out feeling satisfied and wanting to come back for a refill.

READZONE @
A Labyrinthine Aladdin's Cave

MAKE READING A PART OF EVERYONE'S EVERYDAY LIFE

READZONE @ SHISHAN

By 11 A.M. on any Saturday morning, most of the seats in the store—the first community branch run by READZONE—are occupied by parents and children, husbands and wives, students and friends huddled over their book of choice, reading intently by themselves or sharing their thoughts in hushed voices. The bookstore quickly became an integral part of the community, with residents showing no hesitation to call it their own and taking full advantage of the opportunity to be whisked away to a far-away, fairytale land or educated on fascinating topics. The attentive and professional staff treat every small detail with care, making all patrons feel very much at home, as indeed they should in their "community bookstore".

In Zhuhai, the country road not only takes you home, but to a bookstore.

The launch of READZONE in the ancient village of Huitong at the tail end of Chinese Lunar Year, 2017 brought both a first-class collection of reading materials and the bookstore's signature "Southeast Asia Coffee" into the historical village, dubbed "the Cambridge of Zhuhai".

Beautifully adapted to the old-fashioned atmosphere of a hundred-year-old ancestral hall, the bookstore lends a surprising final touch to the overall cultural magnificence of the village with its unique combination of pastoral setting and academic atmosphere created by the development of two vibrant university campuses nearby. The bookstore is rated by the city's book lovers as "the most beautiful country bookstore".

READZONE @ HUITONG VILLAGE

閱潮會同店

AN ENCOUNTER WITH HISTORY

The "bookstore on the island", together with its cozy cafe space, housed in a well appointed corner, greatly enriches the lives of those on the island, linking it in one swoop to all the culture and knowledge that lies beyond its shores.

Brilliantly illustrating what a bookstore can do beyond selling books, it serves as a sanctuary to bring minds and souls together, as well as transport the individual at will, adding cultural luster to the wave beaten facade of the islet. Just like Gabrielle Zevin's phenomenal novel *The Storied Life of A. J. Fikry*, the bookstore is a love letter to the joys of reading, offering sweet therapy for people to combat the sufferings of modern life. Whether the day is sunny or stormy, the nostalgic ambience and pleasant services of the store assistants make it a nice place to curl up with a book and read for hours on end.

" BOOKSTORE ON THE ISLAND "

CHIC, KALEIDOSCOPIC, ARTSY

READZONE @ WAILINGDINGN ISLAND

一切都變得清清楚楚。
除了抵達的道路沒有別的道路。

雖然如此迷人，這島沒人居住，
而在海岸附近看得見的小小腳印
都毫無例外地伸向大海。

彷彿這裏只有離開，
生命那不可測的深處。

維斯瓦娃・辛波絲卡《烏托邦》

The "bookstore on the island" greatly enriches the lives of those on the island, linking it in one swoop to all the culture and knowledge that lies beyond its shores.

WENHUA BOOKSTORE @ YOUNG MIX

HERITAGE AND INNOVATION

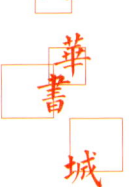

Unveiled in the Gongbei Port neighborhood in 1993 as one of China's first privately-operated bookstores, Wenhua Bookstore now runs a dozen locations across the country. Since it was born, the chain has been taking the lead in the country's bookstore innovation, treating guests with quality coffee and offering a full service venue for a variety of cultural events throughout the year. Over the past two decades, the brand has grown into a lifestyle innovator, against the decreased visibility in print publications. The current 800sqm space on the fourth floor of the Young Mix in downtown Zhuhai offers an oasis of serenity for book loving people in Zhuhai to enjoy the joy of reading.

Lying in the arms of the Tangjiawan Peninsula, on the northern section of the city's Love Promenade, this bookstore is a world of the most beautiful, natural colors and oceanic light. The initial impression is so striking in fact, that it seems to, first, be a dream devised by the designer, and only then a bookstore. It is the city's fairytale, a place that gratifies the senses but also urges the mind to wander and associate freely.

The minimalistic layout of the space draws one's eyes toward the spines of the books, beckoning the visitor to roam mentally and land on the title they desire most. The thick, wooden reading tables provide generous space to enjoy the romantic mood lighting, and the broad windows let in a flood of natural light, allowing the mesmerizing view of the vast sea to cascade in. The lovely facility is completed by an inviting terrace where the wind from the wide-open spaces of the sea, refreshingly but gently, blows all those urban distractions away.

CHIC, KALEIDOSCOPIC, ARTSY

C O A S T   B O O K S T O R E  @

C O A S T   P A R K

Stairway to Knowledge

Xinhua 24-Hour Bookstore @ Wanzaisha

For Those Who Don't Feel Like Going Home

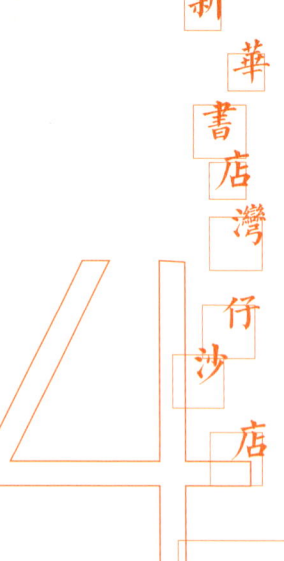

新華書店灣仔沙店

Tied to the theme of "a library for urban night-comers", the bookstore is the Zhuhai version of the 10-episode Japanese live-action television drama *Midnight Diner*, providing locals with a round-the-clock refuge from the break-neck urbanity beyond its doors. Walking into the homey place located on South Fenghuang Road in downtown Zhuhai, one is welcomed by a poster of the TV drama and tempted to read till daybreak. Don't worry. You won't feel lonely here. The city is never short of nightbirds and a loyal night reading contingency.

Shu Sheng Guan @ Hi City

<u>Al fresco and Musical</u>

A trendy venue sited in one of the city's most stylish architectural landmarks on Yeli Island, it is a "musical bookstore" where you may find the vinyl LP you've just been dying to lay your fingers on. The 1,000-square-meter sprawl provides a wonderful children-and-parent zone stuffed full of kids' books and craft stations. The design works to blur the division between indoor spaces and outdoor to create an "al fresco" feel for readers.

One of the lesser-known sides of the city is its nascent filmmaking industry, with its epicenter in the former sugar refinery area of Pingsha. The public is even less familiar with the interesting evolution of "cinematic Zhuhai", which only began to enter the consciousness of movie-goers in 1979, with the release of "A Sweet Career", a romance set in the hard-scrabble world of sugar industry workers in the 1970s.

In 1957, the city's first sugar refinery opened its doors in the undeveloped area of Pingsha and, in 2014, the city's last sugar refinery closed down, marking the end of the city's "sweet age".

In 1980, "A Sweet Career", directed by Xie Tian (1914-2003)—dubbed "China's Charlie Chaplin"—won the Hundred-flower Award, the most prestigious award for TV and filmmakers in China, making Pingsha Refinery a "dream factory".

In 2015, the former refinery site in Pingsha was unveiled as a full-fledged film studio equipped with first-class facilities, awakening the collective memories of the first generation of sugar workers and farmers in Pingsha.

The Return and "Re-purposing" of Pingsha Sugar Refinery

E STORY

Geographically speaking, Pingsha is the hinterland of the Zhuhai port area. Back in Southern Song times, the township with the largest land area in Zhuhai was only a primitive swath of land and several insignificant islets. A thousand years later, Pingsha has become one of the country's key, top-notch yacht manufacturers and home of Zhuhai's first racecourse.

In the modern Chinese historical narrative, Pingsha was a microcosm of New China's vigorous land reform in the 1940s and embodied the famous Chinese saying from that time: "Labor is the most glorious thing". The town's stormy past, together with the toil and blood of the trailblazers, is commemorated by the sculpture at the town's "5.13" Square. In the 1950s, more than 7,000 workers from all across Guangdong Province came to Pingsha to join its reclamation endeavors, led by the 18 founders of the state-owned Pingsha Mechanical Engineering Farm, living in cottages with rampant mosquitoes, enduring hunger and deprivation beyond the imagination of people today.

In the modern Chinese historical narrative, Pingsha was a microcosm of New China's vigorous land reform in the 1940s and embodied the famous Chinese saying from that time: "Labor is a most glorious thing".

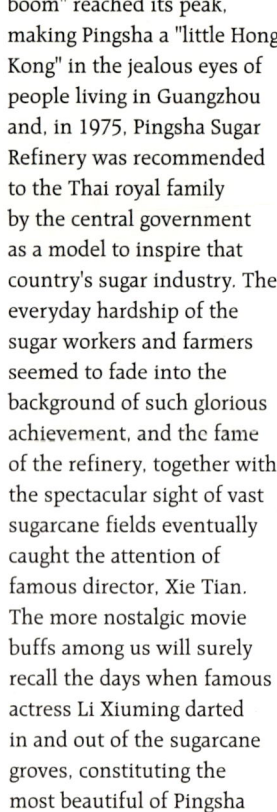

Pingsha Sugar Refinery in the old times

In 1957, with nothing but mangrove and reed forests stretching to the horizon, the Pingsha pioneers tried planting sugarcane on the newly enclosed tideland. The harvest was unexpectedly huge, and Pingsha Sugar Refinery was born. Sugar planting quickly spread into nearby Doumen, Jinwan and present-day Gaolan Port areas, all the way into the farmlands in Nanping Town in southwestern Zhuhai, drawing tens of thousands of farmers and factory workers into the city's "sweet industry", and making sugar farming and processing the cornerstone of Zhuhai's industrial scene.

In the early 1990s, the "sugar boom" reached its peak, making Pingsha a "little Hong Kong" in the jealous eyes of people living in Guangzhou and, in 1975, Pingsha Sugar Refinery was recommended to the Thai royal family by the central government as a model to inspire that country's sugar industry. The everyday hardship of the sugar workers and farmers seemed to fade into the background of such glorious achievement, and the fame of the refinery, together with the spectacular sight of vast sugarcane fields eventually caught the attention of famous director, Xie Tian. The more nostalgic movie buffs among us will surely recall the days when famous actress Li Xiuming darted in and out of the sugarcane groves, constituting the most beautiful of Pingsha

memories. Those "sweet days" were swept up by the rapid urbanization and reorganizing power of industrialization at the beginning of the new millennium, as so often happens in periods of jarring economic change, relegating the proud story of sugar workers in Pingsha to the museum.

The arrival of a TV crew from Beijing in 2013 brought new life to the town's "sweet dream", setting off a process that would build Pingsha into an important part of the country's booming motion picture industry. Impressed by the resilience shown in the town's ever-changing industrial past and the abundantly available local resources for cost-efficient TV and filmmaking, the company decided to invest two billion yuan in the development of Pingsha into a "movie town".

A remake of the former sugar refinery sprawl ensued, resulting in the largest single studio for TV and filmmaking in Asia, ideal for producing Chinese and western vistas—from sea battles to the American Civil War or a Yale University campus in the 19th century. TV and film directors have quickly made the most of the splendid facilities for a range of film and TV genres—from traditional anti-Japanese melodramas to detective operas and historical dramas full of sword-play and intrigue. Nostalgia oozes from every corner of the workshop, and the industrial legacy of Pingsha has added a dozen TV series and films to its roster.

VIII

THE STAIRWAY TO OUTER SPACE
Zhuhai Campus of Sun Yat-sen University (SYSU)

THE "WRITING DESK" OF ZHUHAI
Zhuhai Campus, Jinan University (JNU)

STARRY, STARRY NIGHT
Beijing Normal University, Zhuhai (BNUZ)

HIGH-TABLE DINNER
Beijing Normal University – Hong Kong Baptist University United International College (UIC)

THE LICENSE TO FLY
Beijing Institute of Technology, Zhuhai (BITZH)

TAN IN THE CLASSROOM
Zhuhai College of Jilin University (JLU)

At the Zhuhai Census 2017, the city's population was 1,765,400 including 495,900 students (as of the end of August, 2017). Such a college student proportion leaves most of the other second-tier cities in China far behind. Vocational-technical schools also have a presence that cannot be underestimated in the city's vibrant educational scene. With the number of primary and middle school students counted in, Zhuhai boasts a student population that accounts for roughly one-fourth of the city population, which also means the city is suffering far less from a "graying society" than its peers in China. Statistics also show that these past five years saw an average of some 30,000 college graduates join the city's workforce every year, which means Zhuhai is proud to have a workforce with a higher education qualification far above the national average.

A Cradle of Hi
MY UNI

It is no exaggeration to say Zhuhai, now hosting a dozen prestigious institutions of higher education, is a "university town". The city's stunningly high percentage of the student population injects a steady flow of youthful energy into the bloodstream of the city, with the resulting considerable demographic changes exerting far-reaching impacts beyond the educational genome.

The coastal settlement is a beautiful illustration of how creative minds are fostered by a "green" city and reward the city in many aspects. The city's outstanding farsightedness is fully reflected in the fact that each university campus is set in one of the most scenic locations in Zhuhai. The signature buildings and vistas—Banzhang Mountain of Jinan University, Fenghuang Mountain by the Zhuhai Campus of Sun Yat-sen University, Guanyin Hill at Jilin University's Zhuhai College, along with Chihua Hill near the Zhuhai campus of Beijing Institute of Technology—all contribute significantly to the city's skyline.

A bird's eye view of Zhuhai Campus of Sun Yat-sen University (SYSU)

Beijing Institute of Technology, Zhuhai (BITZH)

*Zh*uhai has five seasons. The fifth season involves its university term times teeming with the breath of youth— the excitement of new arrivals starting their freshman year and the nostalgic joy of graduates parting ways to start a new life.

Although the city's Nanping Village gave birth to the first Chinese student to graduate from an American university, and the consensus that "a city without universities will not have a future" had been long reached, the city's "university boom" did not start until the late 1990s. The first line of the city's "university map" was drawn in 1998, when the Zhuhai campus of Jinan University was unveiled as the city's first full-time university. The next decade saw 10 universities breaking new ground in Zhuhai and bringing some 130,000 students into the city.

The universities, together with their surroundings, are generating a density of high-tech businesses, technology incubators, creative industrial blocks, businesses catering primarily to the university structure, and residential quarters that encompass lovely shopping plazas and set new lifestyle trends for urban dwellers.

The uniqueness of the higher education scene of Zhuhai, however, is not simply a bubble of prestigious names and beautiful campuses. The universities' Zhuhai campuses combine to produce a diverse curriculum, with each having its strength in specific sectors such as information and design at BITZH, translation at Jinan University and its special school open exclusively to overseas Chinese, the "*TianQin*" Project (a space gravitational wave detection research and development project) run by SYSU, the Sino-German cooperation projects of BNU and the inorganic and preparative chemistry program of Jilin University.

Beijing Normal University, Zhuhai (BNUZ), reputed as a "valley university"

The forest campus at the Beijing Normal University, Zhuhai (BNUZ)

Zhuhai Campus of Sun Yat-sen University (SYSU)

The Stairway To Outer Space

Zhuhai Campus of Sun Yat-sen University (SYSU)

A CITY OF LEARNING

> The gigantic structure, together with its rooftop deck, no doubt makes a bold statement that matches the aspiration of Sun Yat-sen, the spiritual incarnation of SYSU.

The library building of the Zhuhai Campus of Sun Yat-sen University looks like two wings fully spread. An imposing stairway of 263 steps set in between the two "wings" seems to be able to reach the sky. At the end of the stairway, the architectural grandeur of the campus opens up in the form of a futuristic rooftop terrace. Standing on this 20,000-square-meter platform, one cannot help wondering how the love-sick who meet for dates on this heavenly terrace locate each other. Well, the students surely have their own romantic ways to tackle the massiveness.

The nondescript, sci-fi aesthetic charm of the campus culminates in its main teaching building, the longest structure of its kind in Asia. Encompassing as many as 179 classrooms of all sizes, the gigantic structure, together with its rooftop deck, no doubt makes a bold statement that matches the aspiration of Sun Yat-sen, the spiritual incarnation of SYSU.

The red-walled one-storey building sitting in parallel with the main teaching building presents a striking contrast to the overbearing cosmic feeling, reminding the more nostalgic visitors of the short-lived but long-remembered National Southwestern Associated University** born in the war flames of 1937. The emerald-green roof set against the cloudless sky has a retro-futuristic vibe.

Standing proudly on Sun Yat-sen Avenue, the bronze statue of Dr. Sun Yat-sen is a replica of the work by Sun's close Japanese friend Umeya Shokichi (1868-1934), the donor of the bronze statue of Sun Yat-sen in SYSU.

As an integral part of the SYSU network, the Zhuhai campus acts as a forerunner in a variety of fields including tourism, international finance, translation and marine sciences.

A new addition of the campus is now under construction. The coastal sprawl across the Gangwan Avenue will evolve into a powerful base of atmospheric and marine sciences, and will be the home ground of the "TianQin" Project, led by SYSU and aiming to lay the cornerstone of China's space gravitational wave detection innovation.

** When the Second Sino-Japanese War broke out between China and Japan in 1937, Peking University, Tsinghua University and Nankai University merged to form Changsha Temporary University in Changsha and later National Southwestern Associated University (Lianda) in Kunming and Mengzi, in Southwest China's Yunnan Province. After the war, the universities moved back and resumed their operation. What was left behind in Kunming became the National Kunming Normal University which later emerged as the Yunnan Normal University.

THE STAIRWAY TO OUTER SPACE

S   U

A CITY OF LEARNING

The "Writing Desk" of Zhuhai

Zhuhai Campus, Jinan University (JNU)

According to Chinese "feng shui" theory, Banzhang Mountain is the "writing desk" of Zhuhai. If the statement holds water, then the Zhuhai campus of Jinan University is the northwest corner of the "desk".

The first piece in the city's "university jigsaw", the campus relocated from Tangjiawan to Qianshan area in 2000. The main road is a green walk clad in dense foliage and stretching from behind the white, European-style, arched gate into the depths of the campus. At the end of the walk is Sun-Moon Lake, obviously wordplay forming an allusion to the Ming (the Chinese character "明" is a combination of "日 sun" and "月 moon") Lake in the university's headquarters in Guangzhou.

Because of the university's special enrollment tradition that dates back to 1906, when the school was based in Nanjing and opened exclusively to Chinese returnees and students from Hong Kong, Macao and Taiwan, the Zhuhai campus is an inheritor of the university's strong Western architectural aesthetics, as can be seen from the arched main gate, the lakeside Baroque-style library and a petite Roman Forum.

The university's library network is so well-established that the resources at each division can be shared not only on an intercollegiate basis but by people outside the university system.

Students at JNU have a lot to brag about, including a highly Westernized campus culture flavored by fairs and festivals rarely found in other universities on the Chinese mainland.

Socrates Café, nestled beside Sun and Moon Lake, is the first entrepreneurial project run solely by JNU Zhuhai students. The café's operating profit goes into the school's special talent cultivation fund and is partly used as relief subsidies and student scholarships.

STARRY, STARRY NIGHT

Beijing Normal University, Zhuhai (BNUZ)

"I know a place, where no one ever goes,
There's peace and quiet, beauty and repose.
It's hidden in a valley, beside a mountain stream,
And lying there beside the stream I find that I can dream."

Our Chalet Songbook, 1981

The culture of the Zhuhai division of Beijing Normal University, dubbed "the most beautiful valley university in Asia", is self-evident. The six gigantic rocks that bear the name of the university in Mao's cursive script calligraphy form a bold declaration of BNUZ's pride, while the sweetness of the valley bespeaks its modesty.

The "gateless" ivory tower cuddling at the foot of the gorgeous Fenghuang Mountain is truly a wonderland of "green and blue" that justifiably ranks among the most beautiful campuses in China. Looking out on a breezy summer day, shadows on the hills sketch the trees and golden phoenix blossoms.

In winter, the daily walk between the dorm buildings—nicknamed the "Potala Palace"—and the classrooms is a heavenly stroll in drifting clouds and mists. The winter chills of southern China feel soothing like an artist's loving hands. The real name of the "Potala Palace" is Jing Hua Yuan, well-known as THE viewing spot for the phantasmagoric spectacle of flaming sunset glow and the dream-like starry sky canopying the "valley campus".

Nature seems to have chosen the valley for wielding its witchcraft. Every day between 9 o'clock and 10 o'clock, the morning sun streaming down through the glass ceiling of the library produces reflections that look like numerous smiling faces, as if presenting a reward to early risers.

Everything in the campus and its surroundings, including the manholes and the name of the university's Sports Department, is an expression of the romanticism of this "fairytale campus".

And what best recommends the "fairyland" is the "BNU blue" that infiltrates the sprawling premise. It is the color of the chairs and desks, of Lotus Lake and Dragonfly Bay, and of the swimming pool set in a man-made sand beach.

Interestingly, the campus road connecting Haihua Zone and Yuehua Zone is named by the students as the "Yue-Hai Expressway".

B N U

Beijing Normal University, Zhuhai

A CITY OF LEARNING

Nature seems to have chosen the valley for wielding its witchcraft.

HIGH-TABLE DINNER

A CITY OF LEARNING

Beijing Normal University – Hong Kong Baptist University United International College (UIC)

The relocation of the Zhuhai campus of UIC from Jinfeng Road, near the Tangjiawan area to the historical Huitong Village in 2017, was not just a geographical change. It was a heaven-made match, just like spring rain soaking into the fields. It is a university setting roots where it originally belonged.

The merger of the village and the elite, higher education institution marks the start of the rise of the Zhuhai version of "Cambridge Town". The watchtowers and ancestral halls from the Qing times came to life. The village's rich historical distillation adds luster to the "blue blood" of UIC and becomes part of the texture of the soul of the university.

A compact estate of only about 20 hectares, the campus serves 6,000 students with a Learning Resources Center that has a seating capacity of 1,800 and more than 150,000 books and journals, all in English. For many UIC graduates, the university's high-table dinner tradition is a most beautiful memory.

Jointly founded by Beijing Normal University and Hong Kong Baptist University (HKBU), it is the first full-scale cooperation in higher education between the Chinese mainland and Hong Kong SAR, shouldering the historical mission of advancing the internationalization of Chinese higher education and taking the lead in implementing liberal arts education in China. Since its first enrollment in 2005, UIC has grown into an international institution with innovative educational approaches.

Teaching staff from more than 30 countries and regions make it possible for UIC to use English as the medium of instruction.

Beijing Normal University - Hong Kong Bapt

UIC's education encourages a high level of student-teacher interaction, mentorship and collaboration. The college takes the lead in implementing Whole Person Education and Four-Point Education, both implemented to realize the college's motto: In knowledge and in deeds, unto the whole person. The school's Whole Person Education works to nurture the inner-self of students so that they can achieve sustained excellence in life and contribute to the betterment of society and the world.

The ethos of Whole Person Education is embedded in the formal and co-curricular learning activities at UIC and realized by students' attainment of seven Graduate Attributes (GAs): Citizenship; Knowledge; Learning; Skills; Creativity; Communication; and Teamwork.

HIGH-TABLE DINNER

University United International College

THE LICENSE TO FLY

Beijing Institute of
Technology, Zhuhai (BITZH)

THE LICENSE TO FLY

A small aeroplane perched in front of the Tianyou Building sets the "masculine" keynote of the Zhuhai division of BIT. The university is one of the country's few higher education institutions that has a well-established School of Aeronautics. The school produces an elite group of 50 pilots each year, much to the jealousy of those who will not have a chance to see their pilot dream come true.

The dominating science and engineering style of the Zhuhai division of BIT can be savored in its "metallic" school facilities that may thwart the faint-hearted. One of the most striking—and formidable—is the school's outdoor training range, where the girls do not have a chance to escape the devilish training on the "deadly slope" and rock-climbing classes.

The school's imposing Ming De Building, sitting on the slope of a hill and overlooking Ming De Lake, looks like a tribute paid to Stanley Kubrick, and wouldn't look out of place in *2001: A Space Odyssey*. With enormous white pillars, the structure is a breath-taking mix of straight lines, smooth white surfaces and endless matrixes. Glistening in the fierce sun of southern China, the chic, neat structure is a strong reminder of the charming "tech-savvy" texture of BIT.

The school's "softness" hiding underneath the "hardness" of the façade takes a little exploration. The "love confession" posts on the school's "BIT (Zhuhai) love board" on WeChat will surely redress one's "science geeks" preconception.

BITZH

Beijing Institute of Technology, Zhuhai

A CITY OF LEARNING

THE LICENSE TO FLY

TAN IN THE CLASSROOM

Zhuhai College of Jilin University (JLU)

L U

Every university campus in Zhuhai has a share of the city's sea view, but the seascape of the Zhuhai division of Jilin University has its unique attractiveness.

In winter, the balmy airstream from the sea and the cold, wet stream from the inland cross swords here. The resulting atmosphere meets with Guanyin Hill lying behind the campus, coagulating into a "bead curtain" that turns the campus into a foggy maze in which even the main gate and campus roads are easy to miss. When the summer heat sets in, the glaring sunbeam cascades through the sparse foliage of coconut trees into the campus. The joint force of strong ultraviolet rays and the sea gusts from the southeast is etched in the tanned skin of the students.

Walk out the main gate, and you'll be instantly inspired by the mesmerising sea view that stretches five kilometers. The South Gate and its surroundings comprise a bustling shopping arcade enjoyed almost exclusively by students and teachers at JLU Zhuhai College.

The inviting coastline within walking distance is not the only thing that makes up for the campus's "out-of-the-way" location that is near the Zhuhai Airport. The university is also the proud owner of the single largest library building in Asia.

High-class sports facilities also recommend the school. For the students here, golfing is an outdoor routine.

Ocean's Bounty

One Night in Zhuhai
Xiawan Food Court & Shuiwan Bar Street

Choice Seafood

Maupassant's Oyster
China's "Oyster Island"

A Taste of Tradition
Doumen's Fascinating Food Culture

OCEAN'S BOUNTY

Care for a taste of China's best groupers, freshest oysters and sea urchins, and the well-kept secret recipe of "seahorse wine" from Dawanshan Island? Zhuhai is a delight for all the senses; and one of the best things to do in the city is gorging on delicious seafood when peering out upon the gentle waves. Speaking fairly, the culinary splendor of the "City of a Hundred Islands" is second to none in China, like a gift that keeps on giving—it rewards the most hypercritical gourmets amongst us with unrivalled seafood from the South China Sea. Sea crabs, jellyfish, squid and numerous exotic forms of sea life regarded as food by humans—the city has got the lot to captivate your taste buds.

Modern times have seen a brilliant fusion of the city's culinary resources and a smorgasbord of styles fostered by a strong immigrant culture, bringing Zhuhai's food culture into an entirely new realm, within which it has ripened into a distinct and comprehensive form that is truly unique in China.

DELICIOUS ZHUHAI

OCEAN'S BOUNTY

Zhuhai justifiably ranks as an important contributor to the culinary spectrum of China's Cantonese region. Ample archaeological evidence has emerged to prove that the ancestors of the Zhuhai people today caught fish and harvested clams to meet basic living needs as early as 4,000 years ago, and that rice growing and pottery-making had become sophisticated enterprises among people living in Housha Bay and Baojing Bay some 6,000 years ago.

The unique mixed tides and moving waters in the estuary bring an abundance of nutrients for aquatic life to thrive, making the region's crabs, white-leg shrimp, sea urchins, squid and oysters the country's most coveted. The waters around many of the city's islands, as exemplified by Miaowan, produce the tastiest seaweed that even the most discerning foodies marvel at.

With the reopening of the fishing season in the South China Sea (after the 3.5 month rehabilitation period from May 1 to August 15) the city's annual seafood spree commences, and this means the following nine months are the best time for foodies to survey the city's various seafood courts and go to Dawanshan Island—far less touristy than many of the other island destinations in Zhuhai—to sample the city's fantastic seafood scene. In fact, seafood lovers who go there will think they have died and gone to heaven.

On the seafood side, the "Zhuhai flavor"

Encounter all kinds of local traditional foods and new culinary trends at Chaoyang Seafood Market.

represents a gourmet philosophy that is rooted in the mastery of "keep it simple and natural", as represented by the locals' decided preference for steamed seafood and "minimalism" in the use of seasonings. The way the most natural flavors of the sea are retained in this cooking process is also the islanders' way of saying thank you to the blessings brought by the sea. Encapsulated in the culinary secrets of Zhuhai, and manifested by the local "fish proverbs" that serves as linguistic reminders of when and how to process the seasonal treats from the ocean, is the islanders' wisdom about the art of timing.

However, this does not mean the chefs here are lacking in creativity. On the contrary, the city's food culture is a reliable source of epicurean surprises when it comes to innovation. Even for the seafood-phobes, there is bound to be something on offer that will grab your fancy.

The locals also excel at making salty, dried fish delicacies that should not be missed. With soup made from fish bone broth, Seafood Rice Noodles is a popular, inexpensive delicacy available at most of the restaurants and food stands across Zhuhai throughout the year.

Travelers are also advised to try the seahorse wine, an invention of the Dawanshan islanders. This strongly herbal liqueur—with its glistening, rosy color—can get you tipsy quicker than you think…

One Night in Zhuhai
Xiawan Food Court & Shuiwan Bar Street

An authentic way to end your Zhuhai trip would be to enjoy the "Zhuhai-style" beer-and-seafood nightlife whilst admiring the charming panorama at one of the many restaurants along the bustling Wanzai Seafood Street. The booths near the Wanzai Wharf area present a dazzling variety of seafood snacks for tourists to sample and buy. Wining and dining here opens your eyes to what the sea really has to offer — a stunning array of sea creatures in all shapes and sizes.

Whether sampling lightly or leaning back into your chair for another belt-busting meal, the nightly riot of sights, smells and sounds at the Xiawan Food Court and Night Market in downtown Zhuhai is perfect for joining the city's authentic midnight food craze. With not only food but shops and vendors' stands, the street is also a great place for people watching and buying souvenirs.

If you feel like a night on the town while in Zhuhai, then you should probably head straight for Shuiwan Street, where a collection of rocking live music bars and their mellow European counterparts are ideal for either dancing or whiling away the long and balmy summer evenings. With regular guest appearances, this lively bar street located in the heart of the bustling Gongbei is live and full of laughter. This block also contains a fine collection of Western-style restaurants and coffee places. Its close proximity to the beautiful shoreline makes it a hotspot for tourists and expats alike.

CHOICE SE

Gou zhua luo
"SEAFOOD FROM HELL"

The small yield of this creepy-looking sea creature in many places in Europe makes it one of the most expensive menu items around, but Wailingding Island in Zhuhai is THE ideal place to try this delicacy that outsiders try so hard to find.

MUSSELS FROM GUISHAN ISLAND
Qingkou

Guishan Island is THE place to indulge in "qingkou" (blue mussels), an edible clam species living on exposed shores in the intertidal zone and attached by means of their strong byssal thread ("beard") to a firm substrate. In traditional Cantonese cuisine, mussels are cooked in a broth of garlic and fermented black bean. Dried mussels are colloquially called "dancai". Wined and dined to satiety, contemporary essayist and translator Liang Shiqiu (1903-1987) confessed his prejudice on the ugliness of the dried clam that "looked like a dehydrated cicada" but actually "tasted indescribably good and unforgettable".

"GENERAL'S HAT" FROM DONG'AO ISLAND
Jiangjun mao

Like each restaurant has its signature dish that you simply must try, the quaintly-named shellfish that looks like a "general's hat" and tastes like the best abalone you can find in this world is an undisputed star on the "Zhuhai seafood menu". The best season to try this delicacy is in winter.

A FOOD

China's "Oyster Island"
MAUPASSANT'S OYSTER

Lee Kum Kee

The reputation of "Hengqin oysters" is closely related to Lee Kum Kee, a Hong Kong-based food company specializing in the manufacture of oyster-flavored sauce and a wide range of Chinese and Asian sauces. The company's purchase of London's landmark Walkie-Talkie skyscraper in 2017 for £1.3bn was a record-breaking transaction for a single building in the UK. Its primary brand, Lee Kum Kee, is popular throughout China and the overseas Chinese community. The company was founded by Lee Kum Sheung, a chef at a small eatery that sold cooked oysters, who is credited with having invented oyster sauce in Nanshui, Zhuhai. In 1888, he formed the Lee Kum Kee company to market what has now become a staple sauce, seasoning and condiment in Cantonese and southern Chinese cuisine. It continues to be run as a family business by his descendants.

The oysters produced in the waters around the city's Hengqin Island present the quintessential example of Nature's Bounty from the South China Sea. Dubbed "the milk from the sea bottom", the oyster is the first marine product to be officially recognized as geographically identified with Zhuhai.

Local chronicles indicate the Song Dynasty saw the rise of the first commercial oyster fishermen on the Zhuhai fishing scene.

Serving as a sustainable (and delectable!) nutrient, oysters play an essential role in the islanders' daily culinary enjoyments, forever inspiring the city's seafaring minds...and stomachs. Oysters can be smoked, boiled, steamed, roasted, barbecued or fried in butter or vegetable oil, and are loaded with nutritious vitamins and minerals, presenting the perfect food from just below the waves, somewhat like the surprise feast given by the pathetic but noble figure, Boule De Suif (Ball of Fat) to her starving comrades in the Maupassant story of the same name. A known lover of the delicious shellfish, oysters found their way into a number of Maupassant's works, but his description in the novel, *Bel Ami*, best reveals his delight: "Small and rich, looking like little ears enfolded in shells, and melting between the palate and the tongue like salted sweets."

Of all the wonderful ways to prepare this super-food notwithstanding, it was the genius of the food-conscious Cantonese that came up with the idea of using chicken soup to boil the oysters fresh from the sea. This cooking method, favored by the more old-fashioned Cantonese, truly ensures the quintessence of this superb bestowment from the sea is perfectly retained.

A TASTE OF TRADITION
Doumen's Fascinating Food Culture

The Doumen District is the city's "vegetable garden and orchard", with its fecund soil and rich water resources ensuring a stable yield of a cornucopia of aquatic products, melons and berries. The region is the source of a host of Zhuhai's most famous local specialties featuring sea bass, Pink Lotus Root, Double-shelled Crab and a dizzying collection of seasonal snacks with queer names, "ya zha bao" (preserved duck bundle) being one of the most famous.

People living in the city's Huangyang area in Doumen are the proud growers of a special breed of "mountain orange". The cultivation of this lovely fruit that is also used to extract fragrant oil from its skin boasts a long history in the village.

Using an odd combination of duck feet, duck chin, duck liver and intestines with fatty pork, the awkward sounding delicacy called "ya zha bao" ranks among the most brilliant representatives of the vibrant food tradition of Doumen District in Zhuhai. The history of this mouthwatering Doumen signature dish, invented by a man eking out a living as a kitchen helper, dates back in the 1940s, when the Hengshan Street enjoyed a reputation of "Little Macao" for its concentration of deli places, restaurants and wet markets.

Another must-try is the Doumen-style Cantonese *cha siu* pork that uses seasonings and a special processing method unique to the Doumen people. And to deny yourself a taste of the "double-shelled" crustacean from Doumen is to miss a rare opportunity, indeed.

Elsewhere, the litchi grown by farmers in Huitong Village enjoys a hard-core clientele.

A TASTE OF TRADITION

NOTES

THIS BOOK

This book was written by Li Jing and David P. Purnell. The project was produced in Hangzhou-based *that's China* office of *that's*:

Project Manager **Alex Zheng**
Managing Writers/Translators **Serene Li, David P. Purnell (U.S.)**
Managing Layout Designer **Serene Li**
Cover Designer **Serene Li**

Internal Photographs Luo Linghao, Wu Guojun, Deng Shuning, Li Jianshu, Zheng Yun, Li Jing, Qiu Ji, He Zhigang, Zhong Fan, Chen Zhi, Xie Ruzhen, Liu Xiaoyan, Yue Shuhua, Zhu Jiang, Xu Xinming, Ruan Yaolin, Zhu Kaiwen, Chen Lixin, Gu Jinlong, Wang Kehong, Feng Bingjia, Lei Wenjun, Li Xuebai, Li Weinian, Liang Lisheng, Ye Yiping, An Dong, Li Jingjing, Zou Jianguo, Lin Yuyun, Liang Genpeng, Xu Fangyun, Liang Senjue, Ou Yi, Li Xuxin, Roser Cervera, Andrew VanderMeulen, Frank Bodenhage, Victor J. Rodriguez, Andrew Webb-Mitchell, Ricardo Mota, Lin Jianjun

Cover photograph Shen Songfa
Back cover photograph Zhang Yonglin, Luo Linghao

Thanks to Information Office of Doumen District of Zhuhai, Gree Group, Huafa Group, Dreamland Hotels & Resorts, Chimelong Ocean Kingdom, Zhuhai Magazine, Zhuhai Museum, COAST Bookstore, COAST Gallery, WUYONG, Beishan World Music Festival, Wenhua Bookstore

All images are copyright of the photographer unless otherwise indicated.

Published by China Intercontinental Press
ISBN 978-7-5085-4032-0

All rights reserved. No part of this publication may be copied, stored in a retrieval system, or transmitted in any form by any means, electronic, mechanical, recording or otherwise, except brief extracts for the purpose of review, and no part of this publication may be sold or hired, without the written permission of the publisher.

Printed through Zhejiang Xinhua Printing Group.
Printed in China.

The producer does not allow its name or logo to be appropriated by commercial establishments, such as retailers, restaurants or hotels. Please let us know of any misuses.

Although the authors have taken all reasonable care in preparing this book, we make no warranty about the accuracy or completeness of its content and, to the maximum extent permitted, disclaim all liability arising from its use.

出　品：	珠海市人民政府新闻办公室
承　制：	五洲传播出版社《城市漫步》全国英文刊 《珠海》杂志有限公司
封面摄影：	沈松发
封底摄影：	张永林　罗令浩
摄　影：	罗令浩　吴国军　邓树宁　李建束　郑昀　厉静 邱戟　何志刚　钟凡　陈智　谢儒侦　刘晓言 岳书华　朱江　许心铭　阮耀林　朱开文　陈立新 谷金龙　汪克宏　冯炳佳　雷文军　李学柏　李伟年 梁力生　叶一屏　安东　李晶晶　邹建国　林裕筠 梁根鹏　许芳芸　梁森爵　欧懿　李绪鑫　Roser Cervera　Andrew VanderMeulen　Frank Bodenhage　Victor J. Rodriguez　Andrew Webb-Mitchell　Ricardo Mota（排列不分先后）

P66页香洲埠老照片由林建军提供

部分图片提供单位：珠海市斗门区新闻办　格力集团　华发集团　静云山庄　长隆海洋王国　《珠海》杂志　珠海市博物馆　无界书店　无界美术馆　无用工作室　北山音乐节　文华书城

如有遗漏或者错误，敬请原谅并及时通知我社。

PRODUCED BY

五洲传播出版社《城市漫步》全国英文刊
**China Intercontinental Press / that's China (magazine)
MULTIFACETED ZHUHAI** 编辑部

ADD: RM. 203, 2/F, BUILDING E, ZHEJIANG DAILY, 178 TIYUCHANG RD., HANGZHOU, ZHEJIANG PROVINCE, CHINA
浙江省杭州市体育场路178号浙江日报社E楼203室　TEL: +86 (571) 87783285, 87783257
JIXITANG2013@163.COM

珠海杂志社有限公司 **Zhuhai Magazine Co., Ltd.**
ADD: 2/F, 297 EAST MEIHUA RD., XIANGZHOU DISTRICT, ZHUHAI, GUANGDONG PROVINCE, CHINA
珠海市香洲区梅华东路297号2楼　TEL: +86 (756) 2639615

图书在版编目（ＣＩＰ）数据

珠海，遇见你 = Multifaceted Zhuhai：英文 / 厉静编著．-- 北京：五洲传播出版社，2018.10
ISBN 978-7-5085-4032-0

Ⅰ．①珠… Ⅱ．①厉… Ⅲ．①珠海－概况－英文 Ⅳ．① K926.53

中国版本图书馆 CIP 数据核字（2018）第 224722 号

MULTIFACETED ZHUHAI

著　者：	厉　静
翻　译：	厉　静
出 版 人：	荆孝敏
策划编辑：	厉　静
责任编辑：	樊程旭
特约编辑：	David P. Purnell（美国）
装帧设计：	厉　静
出版发行：	五洲传播出版社
地　　址：	北京市海淀区北三环中路 31 号生产力大楼 B 座 6 层
邮　　编：	100088
发行电话：	010-82005927，010-82007837
网　　址：	http://www.cicc.org.cn，http://www.thatsbooks.com
印　　刷：	浙江新华数码印务有限公司
版　　次：	2019 年 5 月第 1 版　2019 年 5 月第 1 次印刷
开　　本：	635mm × 965mm　1/32
印　　张：	12.75
字　　数：	150 千字
书　　号：	ISBN 978-7-5085-4032-0
定　　价：	160.00 元

版权所有，侵权必究；如有质量问题，请于印刷厂联系调换。